D0418319

WOE

...ture AQA Anthology

flict

dy Guide

on Level

...de to becoming an expert on
the Anthology part of your GCSE English Literature exam.

It's got everything you need to know — annotated poems,
key themes, exam advice and worked essays.

It's ideal for use as a classroom study book
or a revision guide.

What CGP is all about

Our sole aim here at CGP is to produce the highest quality
books — carefully written, immaculately presented and
dangerously close to being funny.

Then we work our socks off to get them out to you
— at the cheapest possible prices.

CONTENTS

Section Four — Poetry Techniques

Section Five — The Poetry Exam

Section Six — Controlled Assessment

Section Seven — Writing Skills

Published by CGP

Editors:
Edmund Robinson, Edward Robinson, Hayley Thompson, Emma Warhurst
Produced with:
Alison Smith, Peter Thomas, Nicola Woodfin
Contributors:
Caroline Bagshaw, Kevin Smith, Nicola Woodfin

With thanks to Laura Jenkinson and Glenn Rogers for the proofreading
and Jan Greenway for copyright research.

ISBN: 978 1 84762 526 7

Groovy website: www.cgpbooks.co.uk
Jolly bits of clipart from CorelDRAW®
Printed by Elanders Ltd, Newcastle upon Tyne.

Based on the classic CGP style created by Richard Parsons.

How to Use this Book

This guide is for anyone studying the <u>Conflict</u> cluster of the AQA GCSE English Literature <u>Poetry Anthology</u>. You'll have to either answer an <u>exam question</u> on the poems, or write about them for your <u>controlled assessment</u> — your teacher will tell you which.

Sections One and Two are About The Poems

There are usually <u>two pages</u> about <u>each poem</u>. This is what the pages look like:

There's a nice picture of <u>the poet</u> and some info about their life.

Important or tricky bits of the poem are <u>highlighted</u> and <u>explained</u>.

Difficult words are defined in the <u>poem dictionary</u>.

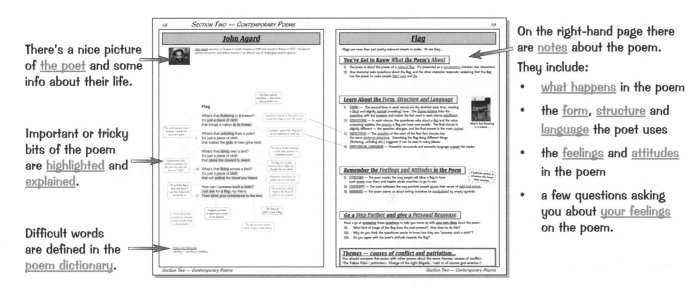

On the right-hand page there are <u>notes</u> about the poem. They include:

- <u>what happens</u> in the poem

- the <u>form</u>, <u>structure</u> and <u>language</u> the poet uses

- the <u>feelings</u> and <u>attitudes</u> in the poem

- a few questions asking you about <u>your feelings</u> on the poem.

If the poem's a bit of a <u>long one</u>, it'll be spread over <u>two pages</u>. One of these will be a <u>pull-out flap</u>. Don't panic. There are full instructions on what to do:

> THIS IS A FLAP.
> FOLD THIS PAGE OUT.

It's Really Important You Know Your Stuff

Whether you're doing the exam or the controlled assessment, you need to be really <u>familiar</u> with the poems.

1) You <u>won't notice</u> everything about a poem on <u>first reading</u>. Keep reading these poems over and over and <u>over again</u>.

2) If you notice something about a poem then <u>jot it down</u> — there's <u>no limit</u> to the number of <u>valid points</u> that could be made about these poems.

3) Make sure you have a go at <u>answering</u> those questions at the bottom of the right-hand page.

> The questions are designed to make you <u>think for yourself</u> about the poems. You'll get <u>marks</u> in both the exam and the controlled assessment for giving <u>your own ideas</u> and <u>opinions</u> on the texts — it's called a <u>personal response</u>.

Nigel's first response to the poems wasn't all that positive.

How to Use this Book

You've got to make <u>comparisons</u> between the poems in your writing — so I've included two dead handy sections showing their <u>similarities</u> and <u>differences</u>. No need to thank me.

Section Three is About Themes and Ideas

This section will help you make <u>links</u> between the <u>themes</u> presented in the poems — it'll give you loads of <u>ideas</u> of what to write about in your exam or controlled assessment.

A <u>different theme</u> is looked at on <u>each page</u>.

Poems which cover the <u>same</u> themes are <u>compared</u>.

Section Four is About Poetry Techniques

1) This section is all about <u>form</u>, <u>structure</u> and <u>language</u>.
2) It looks at how different poets use features like <u>rhyme</u>, <u>rhythm</u> and <u>imagery</u> to create <u>effects</u> — it's something the examiners are <u>dead keen</u> for you to <u>understand</u> and <u>write about</u>.

Each term is <u>explained</u>...

...and looked at in <u>detail</u>.

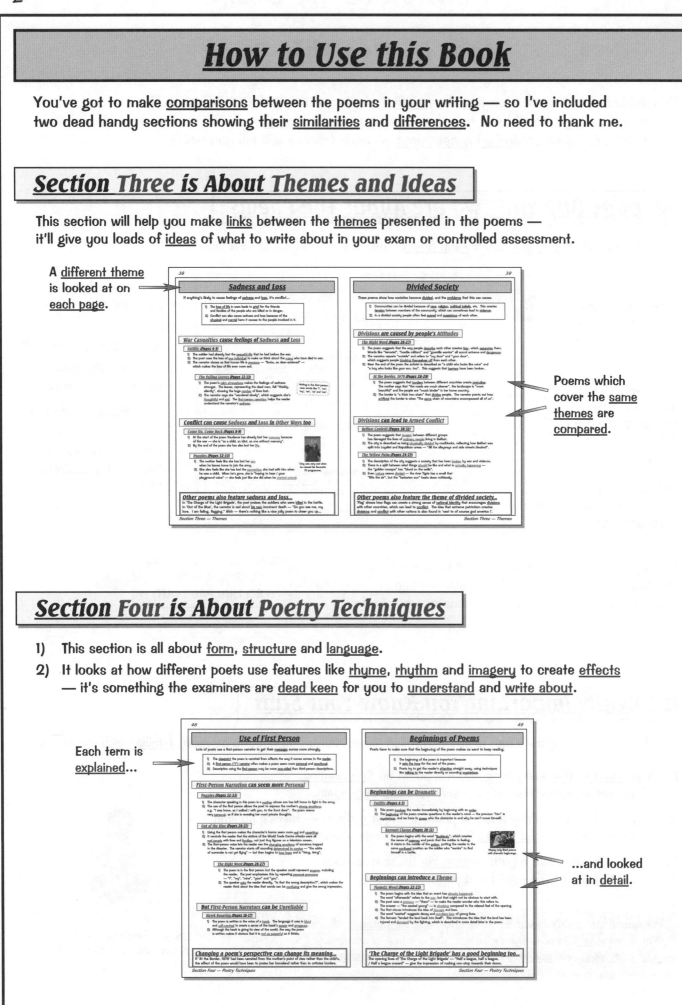

How to Use this Book

If you're studying these poems for the <u>Unit 2 exam</u>, then you need <u>Section Five</u>.
If you're doing these poems for your <u>Unit 5 controlled assessment</u>, look at <u>Section Six</u>.

Section Five Tells You What to Do in Your Exam

This is where you can find out <u>exactly</u> what's involved in your <u>Unit 2: Poetry Across Time</u> exam.

There are <u>questions</u> like the ones you'll get in the exam...

... and <u>sample plans</u> to show you different ways to plan your essay.

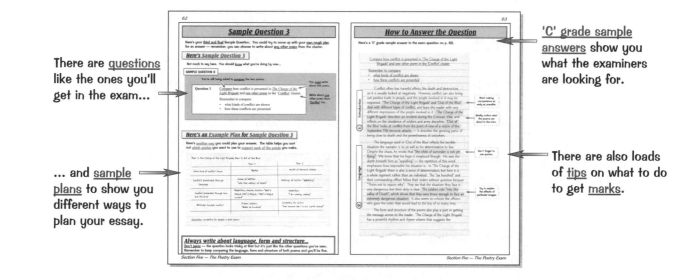

'C' grade sample <u>answers</u> show you what the examiners are looking for.

There are also loads of <u>tips</u> on what to do to get <u>marks</u>.

Section Six Tells You What to Do in Your Controlled Assessment

This section gives you the lowdown on the <u>Unit 5: Exploring Poetry</u> controlled assessment.

There are some <u>example questions</u> like the ones you'll be given, as well as...

...tips on <u>planning</u> and <u>preparing</u> for your assessment piece...

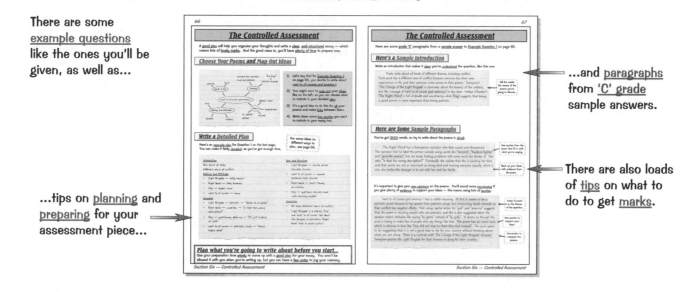

...and <u>paragraphs</u> from '<u>C</u>' grade sample answers.

There are also loads of <u>tips</u> on what to do to get <u>marks</u>.

Section Seven Helps You Improve Your Writing Skills

1) This section gives you some great tips on <u>how to answer</u> the question <u>well</u>.

2) There are some useful pointers for writing a <u>good essay</u> too —
   including advice on <u>quoting</u> and <u>paragraphs</u>. You'll find it dead helpful.

Wilfred Owen

<u>Wilfred Owen</u> (1893-1918) was born in Shropshire to an English and Welsh family and was best known for his war poems written whilst he served in the trenches in World War One.
He died in battle only one week before the end of the war.

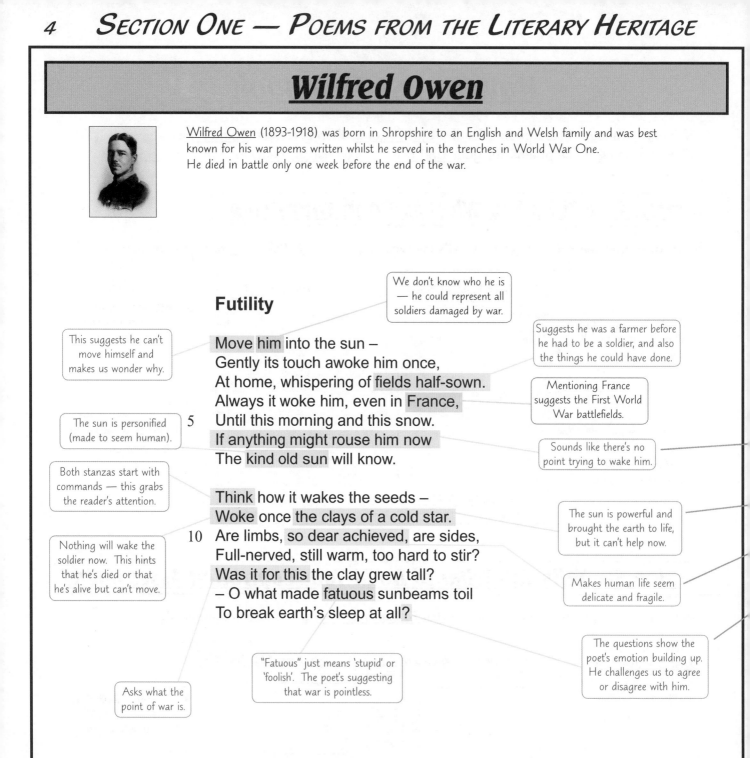

Futility

Move him into the sun –
Gently its touch awoke him once,
At home, whispering of fields half-sown.
Always it woke him, even in France,
5   Until this morning and this snow.
If anything might rouse him now
The kind old sun will know.

Think how it wakes the seeds –
Woke once the clays of a cold star.
10   Are limbs, so dear achieved, are sides,
Full-nerved, still warm, too hard to stir?
Was it for this the clay grew tall?
– O what made fatuous sunbeams toil
To break earth's sleep at all?

Annotations:

We don't know who he is — he could represent all soldiers damaged by war.

This suggests he can't move himself and makes us wonder why.

Suggests he was a farmer before he had to be a soldier, and also the things he could have done.

Mentioning France suggests the First World War battlefields.

The sun is personified (made to seem human).

Sounds like there's no point trying to wake him.

Both stanzas start with commands — this grabs the reader's attention.

The sun is powerful and brought the earth to life, but it can't help now.

Nothing will wake the soldier now. This hints that he's died or that he's alive but can't move.

Makes human life seem delicate and fragile.

The questions show the poet's emotion building up. He challenges us to agree or disagree with him.

Asks what the point of war is.

"Fatuous" just means 'stupid' or 'foolish'. The poet's suggesting that war is pointless.

POEM DICTIONARY
futility — uselessness
rouse — wake
stir — begin to wake up
fatuous — unthinkingly foolish
toil — work hard

Futility

This is quite a depressing poem. But then, with a cluster called "conflict", what did you expect?

You've Got to Know What the Poem's About

1) The poem is about an <u>injured</u>, probably <u>dead</u>, <u>soldier</u>.
2) It's set in <u>France</u> during the <u>First World War</u>.
3) The poet questions what the <u>point</u> is of <u>life</u> being <u>created</u> if it can be <u>destroyed</u> so easily.

Learn About the Form, Structure and Language

1) <u>FORM</u> — The poet mainly uses <u>half-rhyme</u>, which makes the poem seem <u>less formal</u> and more <u>natural</u>.
2) <u>STRUCTURE</u> — Each stanza begins with a <u>command</u>. The first stanza describes how to help the soldier. In the second stanza the language is more <u>thoughtful</u>.
3) <u>PAST AND PRESENT</u> — The poet talks about things in both the <u>past</u> and the <u>present</u>. This shows the <u>contrast</u> between the soldier's life at home and at war. The repeated descriptions of <u>waking</u> emphasise the <u>contrast</u> between being awake and alive and being paralysed or dead.
4) <u>PERSONIFICATION</u> — <u>Nature</u> is personified as <u>powerful</u>, but <u>helpless</u> in the face of war.
5) <u>PHILOSOPHICAL LANGUAGE</u> — In the second stanza the poet asks whether creation is <u>worthwhile</u> when life can be <u>ended</u> so quickly.
6) <u>DIRECT LANGUAGE</u> — The poet addresses the <u>reader</u> directly, which makes the reader feel more <u>emotionally involved</u> with the poem.

Remember the Feelings and Attitudes in the Poem

1) <u>SYMPATHY</u> — The poet is <u>sympathetic</u> to the soldier, and uses a <u>kind</u> and <u>respectful</u> tone to talk about him.
2) <u>ANGER</u> — The poet feels <u>bitter</u> about the <u>waste of life</u> caused by war. He's <u>frustrated</u> at how <u>pointless</u> it is to create life when it's <u>destroyed</u> by war.

Go a Step Further and give a Personal Response

Have a go at <u>answering</u> these <u>questions</u> to help you come up with <u>your own ideas</u> about the poem:

Q1. Is the soldier dead, injured or dying? What clues are there in the poem?
Q2. How does the title of the poem relate to what happens in it?
Q3. What can you tell about the poet's attitude to war, and do you agree with it?

Themes — effects of conflict, sadness and loss, helplessness...

You should compare this poem with other poems about the same themes: sadness and loss: 'The Falling Leaves', 'Come On, Come Back'; effects of conflict: 'Poppies'; helplessness: 'Belfast Confetti'.

Section One — Poems from the Literary Heritage

Alfred Tennyson

The cavalry only had swords against the Russian guns.

Could mean that people wondered why they had been sent on the charge (or how they could be so brave).

The alliteration here makes the battle sound terrifying.

The repetition of "Flash'd" and the rhyme create a powerful image of the cavalry using their swords.

They kept going even through a blinding wall of gun smoke — this shows their courage.

It's clear that some of them have been killed.

4.

Flash'd all their sabres bare,
Flash'd as they turn'd in air
Sabring the gunners there,
30 Charging an army, while
     All the world wonder'd:
Plunged in the battery-smoke
Right thro' the line they broke;
Cossack and Russian
35 Reel'd from the sabre stroke
     Shatter'd and sunder'd.
Then they rode back, but not
     Not the six hundred.

Similar to the opening lines of stanza 3, but now the soldiers are retreating.

The repetition reminds us that lives have been lost, and makes the poem sound sad.

The sense of admiration is touched with sadness.

5.

Cannon to right of them,
40 Cannon to left of them,
Cannon behind them
     Volley'd and thunder'd;
Storm'd at with shot and shell,
While horse and hero fell,
45 They that had fought so well
Came thro' the jaws of Death
Back from the mouth of Hell,
All that was left of them,
     Left of six hundred.

A rhetorical question is a question designed to make people think — but that isn't really meant to be answered.

Sounds dramatic and daring.

This command is repeated to tell us we should honour the cavalry.

This is a rhetorical question that challenges the reader.

Repeated from stanza 4 — it emphasises people's amazement at their bravery.

6.

50 When can their glory fade?
O the wild charge they made!
     All the world wonder'd.
Honour the charge they made!
Honour the Light Brigade,
55   Noble six hundred!

The poet wants the cavalry to be remembered, including the ones who died.

POEM DICTIONARY
league — an old measurement of distance (about 3 miles long)
sabre — a type of sword with a curved blade
battery-smoke — the smoke from the groups of enemy cannons
Cossack — a warrior from southern Russia and Ukraine
sunder'd — broken apart
volley'd — fired several shells at the same time

Alfred Tennyson

Alfred Tennyson (1809-1892) was born in Lincolnshire and later lived on the Isle of Wight and in Surrey. He studied at Trinity College, Cambridge. Tennyson was one of the great poets of the Victorian era and was Poet Laureate from 1850 to 1892.

The Charge of the Light Brigade

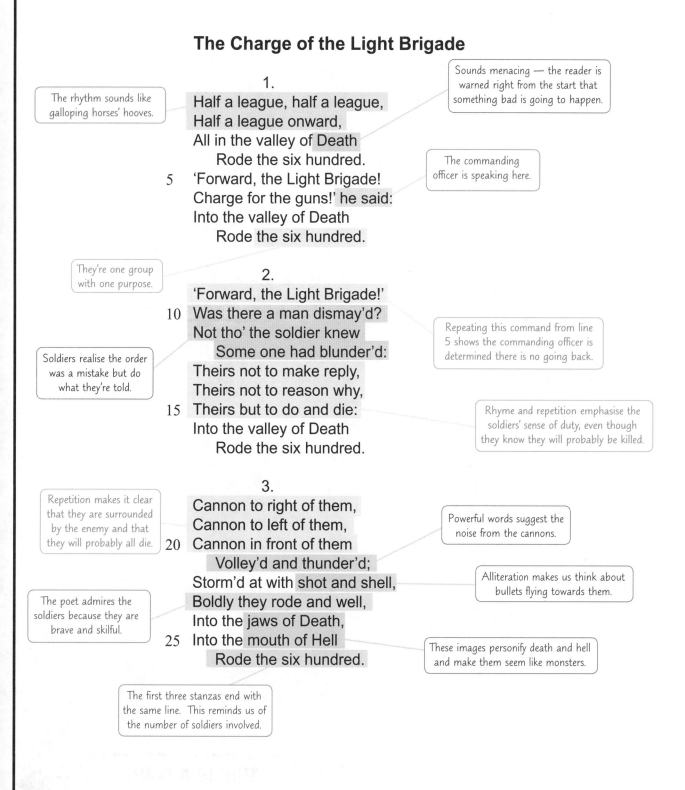

1.

Half a league, half a league,
Half a league onward,
All in the valley of Death
    Rode the six hundred.
5 'Forward, the Light Brigade!
Charge for the guns!' he said:
Into the valley of Death
    Rode the six hundred.

2.

'Forward, the Light Brigade!'
10 Was there a man dismay'd?
Not tho' the soldier knew
    Some one had blunder'd:
Theirs not to make reply,
Theirs not to reason why,
15 Theirs but to do and die:
Into the valley of Death
    Rode the six hundred.

3.

Cannon to right of them,
Cannon to left of them,
20 Cannon in front of them
    Volley'd and thunder'd;
Storm'd at with shot and shell,
Boldly they rode and well,
Into the jaws of Death,
25 Into the mouth of Hell
    Rode the six hundred.

The rhythm sounds like galloping horses' hooves.

Sounds menacing — the reader is warned right from the start that something bad is going to happen.

The commanding officer is speaking here.

They're one group with one purpose.

Repeating this command from line 5 shows the commanding officer is determined there is no going back.

Soldiers realise the order was a mistake but do what they're told.

Rhyme and repetition emphasise the soldiers' sense of duty, even though they know they will probably be killed.

Repetition makes it clear that they are surrounded by the enemy and that they will probably all die.

Powerful words suggest the noise from the cannons.

Alliteration makes us think about bullets flying towards them.

The poet admires the soldiers because they are brave and skilful.

These images personify death and hell and make them seem like monsters.

The first three stanzas end with the same line. This reminds us of the number of soldiers involved.

THIS IS A FLAP.
FOLD THIS PAGE OUT.
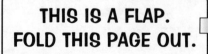

The Charge of the Light Brigade

This one's based on a real battle from the Crimean War, where a commanding officer gave an order that led to most of his soldiers ending up dead. Oops...

You've Got to Know What the Poem's About

1) The poem describes a <u>battle</u> between <u>British cavalry</u> (soldiers on horseback) and <u>Russian forces</u> during the <u>Crimean War</u> (1853-1856).

2) A <u>misunderstanding</u> meant that the Light Brigade was ordered to <u>ride</u> into a valley surrounded by <u>enemy soldiers</u>.

3) The cavalry were only armed with <u>swords</u>, but the Russian soldiers had <u>guns</u>. The Light Brigade were <u>outnumbered</u> by the enemy, and many of them were <u>killed</u>.

Learn About the Form, Structure and Language

1) <u>FORM</u> — The poem is narrated in the <u>third person</u> (the narrator tells the story but they were not actually involved in it), using words like 'they' and 'them'. There's a strong, regular <u>rhythm</u> that creates a fast pace with the cavalry <u>galloping forward</u>.

2) <u>STRUCTURE</u> — The poem describes the battle in <u>chronological order</u> (the order it happened). Some lines and phrases are <u>repeated</u> throughout the poem, keeping the reader focused on the <u>cavalry troops</u>.

3) <u>REPETITION</u> — Repetition shows that something bad is going to happen. Repetition of "<u>the six hundred</u>" in each stanza reminds us of the <u>large numbers</u> of men involved and the <u>chaos</u> of the battle.

4) <u>VIOLENT LANGUAGE</u> — The poet chooses <u>powerful</u> words to describe the <u>violence</u> of the battle.

5) <u>HEROIC LANGUAGE</u> — The poet uses <u>respectful</u> language to emphasise the soldiers' <u>bravery</u> and <u>heroism</u>.

Remember the Feelings and Attitudes in the Poem

1) <u>ADMIRATION</u> — The poet admires the <u>bravery</u> and <u>sacrifice</u> of the men. They were determined to <u>obey orders</u> even though they knew death was likely.

2) <u>DISBELIEF</u> — The poet seems shocked by the <u>stupidity</u> of the order, but he still <u>respects</u> the soldiers who did their duty.

3) <u>HORROR</u> — The poet is horrified by the <u>violence</u> of the battle.

Go a Step Further and give a Personal Response

Have a go at <u>answering</u> these <u>questions</u> to help you come up with <u>your own ideas</u> about the poem:

Q1. How does the poet show the reader that he admires and respects the cavalry troops?

Q2. What techniques does the poet use to show how terrifying and violent the battle was?

Q3. What impression does the poem give of the commanding officers?

Themes — effects of conflict, reality of battles, patriotism...

You can compare this poem with other poems about the same themes: effects of conflict: 'Poppies', 'Futility'; reality of battles: 'Bayonet Charge'; patriotism: 'next to of course god america i'.

Stevie Smith

Repeating this word makes the sense of doom stronger.

Personification of the undercurrent adds to the creepy atmosphere.

Weeping bitterly for her ominous mind, her plight,
Up the river of white moonlight she swims
30 Until a treacherous undercurrent
Seizing her in an icy-amorous embrace
Dives with her, swiftly severing
The waters which close above her head.

This is an oxymoron. "Icy" and "amorous" would normally seem like opposites.

Alliteration emphasises the speed of what is happening.

Alliteration emphasises the time passing slowly.

An enemy sentinel
35 Finding the abandoned clothes
Waits for the swimmer's return
('Come on, come back')
Waiting, whiling away the hour
Whittling a shepherd's pipe from the hollow reeds.

This is the title of a song.

A strangely innocent image for a soldier waiting to kill someone.

There are no brackets around the song title this time — it's as if the music is getting louder.

40 In the chill light of dawn
Ring out the pipe's wild notes
'Come on, come back.'

It's ironic that Vaudevue sang the same song as her enemy.

Vaudevue
In the swift and subtle current's close embrace
45 Sleeps on, stirs not, hears not the familiar tune
Favourite of all the troops of all the armies
Favourite of Vaudevue
For she had sung it too
Marching to Austerlitz,
50 'Come on, come back.'

Enemies have some things in common.

Reminds the reader of the beginning of the poem, when Vaudevue had just survived the battle.

The poem ends sadly — Vaudevue won't come back because she's dead.

POEM DICTIONARY
Memel — a real town in Nazi Germany, now in Lithuania
M.L.5. — an imaginary weapon (possibly a poisonous gas)
hummock — a little hill
rutted — uneven or bumpy
profound — 'deep' and meaningful
ominous — suggesting that something bad is going to happen
treacherous — severe, dangerous or betraying
amorous — loving
embrace — grip, clutch, hold
sentinel — a guard or lookout

Stevie Smith

<u>Stevie Smith</u> (1902-1971), real name 'Florence', was born in Kingston upon Hull, but spent most of her life living in North London with her aunt, working for Newnes Publishing Company. She was awarded the Queen's Gold Medal for Poetry in 1969.

'Come On, Come Back'

Incident in a future war

> The poem's set in the future, so the story is made up.

Left by the ebbing tide of battle
On the field of Austerlitz

> There was a real battle in Austerlitz in 1805.

The girl soldier Vaudevue sits

> The unusual combination of her being a girl and a soldier sounds like a contradiction.

Her fingers tap the ground, she is alone

> Repeated for emphasis.

5   At midnight in the moonlight she is sitting alone on a round flat stone.

> Alliteration creates a creepy, eerie setting.

Graded by the Memel Conference first
Of all human exterminators
M.L.5.

> The imaginary conference on killing suggests how seriously war is still taken in the future.

Has left her just alive

> She's clearly shocked by what's happened.

10   Only her memory is dead for evermore.

> This is a scary word.

She fears and cries, Ah me why am I here?
Sitting alone on a round flat stone on a hummock there.

> When two words that rhyme are in the same line, it's called 'internal rhyme'.

Rising, staggering, over the ground she goes
Over the seeming miles of rutted meadow

> The ground is difficult to walk over — this contrasts with the sand at the end of the stanza.

15   To the margin of a lake
The sand beneath her feet
Is cold and damp and firm to the waves' beat.

> The sand is firm, but Vaudevue is fragile.

Quickly – as a child, an idiot, as one without memory –
She strips her uniform off, strips, stands and plunges
20   Into the icy waters of the adorable lake.

> It seems strange to say that the lake is both "icy" and "adorable". This makes the reader feel confused, like Vaudevue.

On the surface of the water lies
A ribbon of white moonlight

> A peaceful image. The moon creates a dreamy feel.

The waters on either side of the moony track
Are black as her mind,
25   Her mind is as secret from her
As the water on which she swims,
As secret as profound as ominous.

> She doesn't know what's happening or what she's doing.

> Ending the stanza with this word hints that something bad will happen.

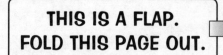

THIS IS A FLAP. FOLD THIS PAGE OUT.

'Come On, Come Back'

Another poem about war. This one's set in the future though, which might make it a bit different. Maybe.

You've Got to Know What the Poem's About

1) The poem is about a <u>young female soldier</u>, Vaudevue. She has just fought in a <u>battle</u> at Austerlitz.

2) She is alive but she has been badly <u>injured</u> and has lost her <u>memory</u>, so she's very <u>confused</u>.

3) Vaudevue is so <u>upset</u> that she suddenly strips off and <u>jumps</u> into the <u>lake</u>.

4) An <u>enemy soldier</u> finds Vaudevue's clothes and <u>waits</u> for her to come back.
Vaudevue <u>doesn't</u> come back though because she is <u>already dead</u>.

Learn About the Form, Structure and Language

1) <u>FORM</u> — The line lengths are a <u>mixture</u> of short and long, which creates
a rambling effect. The irregular <u>rhyme</u> and <u>internal rhyme</u> makes us
<u>uncomfortable</u>. It makes the reader <u>confused</u>, just like Vaudevue.

2) <u>STRUCTURE</u> — The events in the poem are told in <u>chronological order</u> (the order they
happen in). The last three lines of the poem link back to the battle at the start.

3) <u>REPETITION</u> — Repeating the title <u>song</u> reminds the reader of <u>all</u> who have been lost,
not just Vaudevue. <u>Key words</u> are also <u>repeated</u> to give the poem a <u>cold</u>, <u>deathly</u> feel.

4) <u>SURREAL LANGUAGE</u> — Strong <u>descriptive images</u> and <u>personification</u> create a <u>creepy</u> atmosphere.

5) <u>PAST AND FUTURE</u> — There are several references to places associated with past wars.
There are references to <u>war</u> in both the <u>past</u> and <u>future</u>, suggesting that there will <u>always</u> be war.

Remember the Feelings and Attitudes in the Poem

1) <u>IMPERSONAL ATTITUDE</u> — The narrative voice is very <u>impersonal</u> (we don't see the
narrator's emotions), even though what happens in the poem is very <u>dramatic</u>.

2) <u>IRONY</u> — It's <u>ironic</u> that Vaudevue and her enemy have the <u>same favourite song</u>.

3) <u>MYSTERY</u> — The poem has some mysterious elements like <u>moonlight</u> and <u>pipe music</u>.

Go a Step Further and give a Personal Response

Have a go at <u>answering</u> these <u>questions</u> to help you come up with <u>your own ideas</u> about the poem:

Q1.　How do you think that the poet helps the reader to relate to Vaudevue's state of confusion?

Q2.　What does the poet make you think about the enemy sentinel in the poem?

Q3.　Do you think that the poet's vision of the future in this poem is realistic?

Themes — death, sadness and loss...

You should compare this poem with other poems about the same themes: sadness and loss: 'Futility',
'The Falling Leaves', 'Poppies'; death: 'Out of the Blue', 'Mametz Wood', 'Hawk Roosting'.

10

Ted Hughes

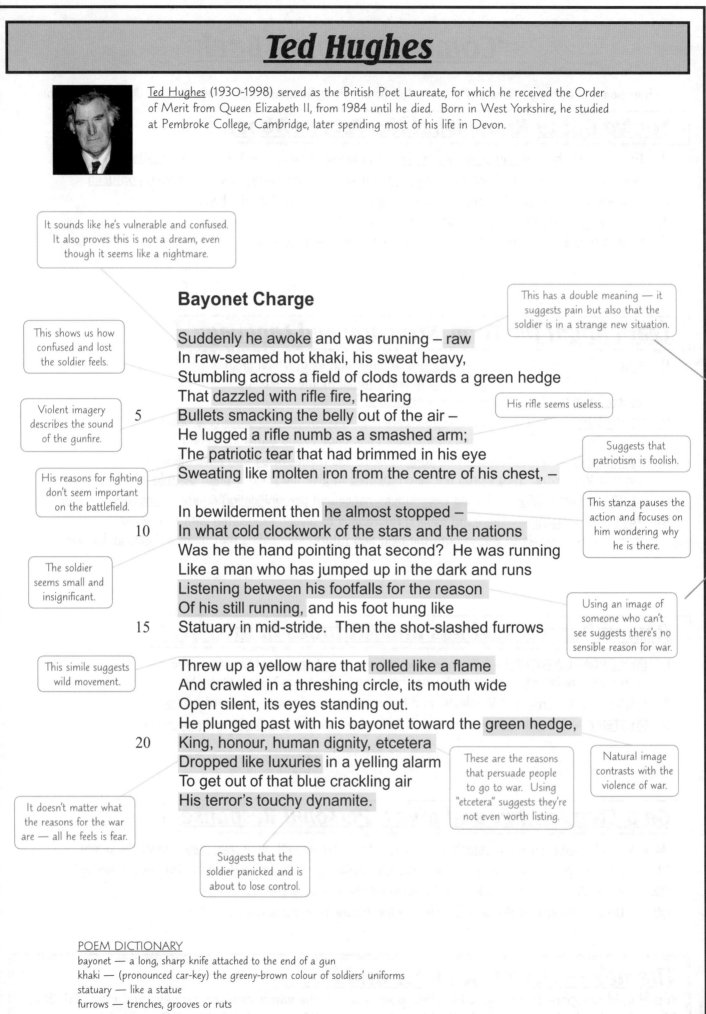

Ted Hughes (1930-1998) served as the British Poet Laureate, for which he received the Order of Merit from Queen Elizabeth II, from 1984 until he died. Born in West Yorkshire, he studied at Pembroke College, Cambridge, later spending most of his life in Devon.

It sounds like he's vulnerable and confused. It also proves this is not a dream, even though it seems like a nightmare.

Bayonet Charge

This has a double meaning — it suggests pain but also that the soldier is in a strange new situation.

This shows us how confused and lost the soldier feels.

Violent imagery describes the sound of the gunfire.

His reasons for fighting don't seem important on the battlefield.

The soldier seems small and insignificant.

This simile suggests wild movement.

It doesn't matter what the reasons for the war are — all he feels is fear.

His rifle seems useless.

Suggests that patriotism is foolish.

This stanza pauses the action and focuses on him wondering why he is there.

Using an image of someone who can't see suggests there's no sensible reason for war.

These are the reasons that persuade people to go to war. Using "etcetera" suggests they're not even worth listing.

Natural image contrasts with the violence of war.

Suggests that the soldier panicked and is about to lose control.

Suddenly he awoke and was running – raw
In raw-seamed hot khaki, his sweat heavy,
Stumbling across a field of clods towards a green hedge
That dazzled with rifle fire, hearing
5 Bullets smacking the belly out of the air –
He lugged a rifle numb as a smashed arm;
The patriotic tear that had brimmed in his eye
Sweating like molten iron from the centre of his chest, –

In bewilderment then he almost stopped –
10 In what cold clockwork of the stars and the nations
Was he the hand pointing that second? He was running
Like a man who has jumped up in the dark and runs
Listening between his footfalls for the reason
Of his still running, and his foot hung like
15 Statuary in mid-stride. Then the shot-slashed furrows

Threw up a yellow hare that rolled like a flame
And crawled in a threshing circle, its mouth wide
Open silent, its eyes standing out.
He plunged past with his bayonet toward the green hedge,
20 King, honour, human dignity, etcetera
Dropped like luxuries in a yelling alarm
To get out of that blue crackling air
His terror's touchy dynamite.

POEM DICTIONARY
bayonet — a long, sharp knife attached to the end of a gun
khaki — (pronounced car-key) the greeny-brown colour of soldiers' uniforms
statuary — like a statue
furrows — trenches, grooves or ruts

Bayonet Charge

If you've ever thought that being in a war sounds like fun, this poem might change your mind.

You've Got to Know *What* the Poem's *About*

1) The poem is about a soldier's experience of a <u>battle</u>. It describes his thoughts and actions as he desperately tries to <u>avoid</u> being <u>shot</u>.

2) The soldier's main emotion is <u>fear</u>, which has replaced the more <u>patriotic thoughts</u> that he had before the violence began.

Learn About the *Form, Structure and Language*

1) <u>FORM</u> — The poet uses a lot of <u>enjambment</u> (where phrases <u>run over</u> onto the line below). There is no rhyme scheme, which emphasises the <u>confusion</u> of the soldier as he <u>stumbles</u> forward.

2) <u>STRUCTURE</u> — The poem starts in the <u>middle of the action</u> and focuses on the soldier's actions and thoughts. The middle stanza describes a <u>pause</u> — time seems to <u>stand still</u> and the soldier's <u>confusion</u> turns to <u>terror</u>. The last stanza returns to <u>panicked movement</u> as he runs for safety.

3) <u>UNIVERSAL LANGUAGE</u> — The poet keeps the soldier <u>anonymous</u> (unnamed). It suggests that he is a <u>universal</u> figure who could represent <u>any</u> young soldier.

4) <u>IMAGERY</u> — The poet uses powerful <u>imagery</u> to show the <u>horror</u> of war.

5) <u>VIOLENT LANGUAGE</u> — There is some shocking and brutal imagery to bring home the sights and sounds of war. This helps to convey the sense of <u>confusion</u> and <u>fear</u> to the reader more strongly.

Remember the *Feelings and Attitudes in the Poem*

Not that kind of terror...

1) <u>TERROR</u> — The poem <u>challenges patriotism</u> and shows how <u>terror</u> becomes the main emotion in battle.

2) <u>CONFUSION</u> — The soldier is confused because he's <u>disorientated</u> by the gunfire, but he's also <u>questioning</u> what he's doing there at all.

Go a *Step Further* and give a *Personal Response*

Have a go at <u>answering</u> these <u>questions</u> to help you come up with <u>your own ideas</u> about the poem:

Q1. How does the middle stanza differ from the other two stanzas?

Q2. How does the poet show the confusion in the poem?

Q3. What does the poem suggest about the poet's attitude to war?

Themes — *effects of conflict, reality of battles, nature...*

You should compare this poem with other poems about the same themes: effects of conflict: 'The Charge of the Light Brigade', 'Poppies'; reality of battles: Belfast Confetti; nature: 'Mametz Wood'.

Margaret Postgate Cole

Dame Margaret Postgate Cole (1893-1980) was an English politician and writer who campaigned against conscription during the First World War. She studied at Cambridge and worked as a teacher whilst writing, before entering politics in 1941 specialising in education.

The Falling Leaves

November 1915

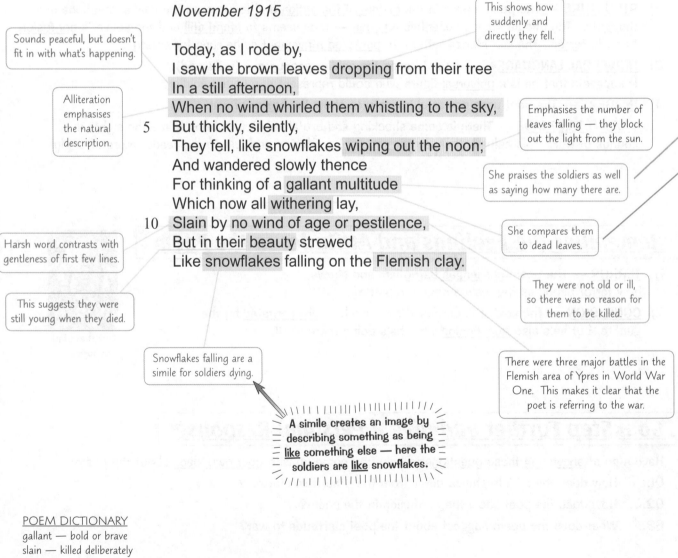

Today, as I rode by,
I saw the brown leaves dropping from their tree
In a still afternoon,
When no wind whirled them whistling to the sky,
5   But thickly, silently,
They fell, like snowflakes wiping out the noon;
And wandered slowly thence
For thinking of a gallant multitude
Which now all withering lay,
10 Slain by no wind of age or pestilence,
But in their beauty strewed
Like snowflakes falling on the Flemish clay.

Annotations:

Sounds peaceful, but doesn't fit in with what's happening.

This shows how suddenly and directly they fell.

Alliteration emphasises the natural description.

Emphasises the number of leaves falling — they block out the light from the sun.

She praises the soldiers as well as saying how many there are.

She compares them to dead leaves.

Harsh word contrasts with gentleness of first few lines.

This suggests they were still young when they died.

They were not old or ill, so there was no reason for them to be killed.

Snowflakes falling are a simile for soldiers dying.

A simile creates an image by describing something as being *like* something else — here the soldiers are *like* snowflakes.

There were three major battles in the Flemish area of Ypres in World War One. This makes it clear that the poet is referring to the war.

POEM DICTIONARY
gallant — bold or brave
slain — killed deliberately
pestilence — a disease
strewed — spread out or scattered carelessly
Flemish — from the Flanders region, which covers parts of Belgium, France and the Netherlands

The Falling Leaves

'What's a poem about leaves doing in a book about war poetry?', you might be wondering. Good question. But things aren't quite as they seem...

You've Got to Know What the Poem's About

1) The poem is about <u>autumn leaves</u> falling from the trees.
2) The falling leaves remind the poet of young <u>soldiers</u> being <u>killed</u> in war.

Learn About the Form, Structure and Language

1) <u>FORM</u> — The poem is made up of <u>one stanza</u>, which contains only <u>one sentence</u>. The <u>line lengths</u> vary, showing the <u>random</u> way that leaves fall. The regular <u>rhyme scheme</u> helps to create a <u>peaceful</u> mood.

2) <u>STRUCTURE</u> — The poem is centred around the end of <u>line 6</u> — before this the poet is describing the <u>leaves falling</u> for no reason, and afterwards she switches to describing <u>soldiers</u> being pointlessly <u>killed</u>.

3) <u>FORMAL LANGUAGE</u> — The poet uses quite <u>formal</u> words in the poem. This shows that the poem has a <u>serious message</u> about <u>death</u> and <u>war</u>.

4) <u>NATURAL IMAGERY</u> — Falling leaves and dying men are both compared to <u>snowflakes</u>. This highlights the huge <u>number</u> of men killed in such a short amount of time. There is some <u>alliteration</u> to describe <u>natural</u> details like wind and snow.

Remember the Feelings and Attitudes in the Poem

1) <u>SADNESS</u> — The poem has a <u>calm</u>, <u>thoughtful</u> tone of sadness as the poet imagines the large numbers of soldiers <u>killed</u> by war.

2) <u>REGRET</u> — There's a sense of sorrow for the <u>deaths</u> that have happened for <u>no clear reason</u>.

3) <u>RESPECT</u> — The poet shows respect for those who gave their <u>lives</u> in the war.

Margaret loved falling leaves — especially if they had poems on them.

Go a Step Further and give a Personal Response

Have a go at <u>answering</u> these <u>questions</u> to help you come up with <u>your own ideas</u> about the poem:

Q1.   How does the poet create an atmosphere of sadness in the poem?

Q2.   Why do you think the poet uses the simile of snowflakes in the poem?

Q3.   How do you think the poet feels about the war, and how does she show this in the poem?

Themes — death, sadness and loss...

You should compare this poem with other poems about the same themes: death: 'Out of the Blue', 'Mametz Wood', 'Come On, Come Back'; sadness and loss: 'Futility', 'Poppies'.

E E Cummings

Edward Estlin Cummings (1894-1962) was an American poet, born in Massachusetts, who studied at Harvard University and later travelled in Europe and North Africa throughout the 1920s and 1930s.

The speaker knows what he's expected to say. He links America with God, to please listeners.

The speaker can't be bothered to be specific.

He doesn't sound very committed here.

Scraps of lines from the patriotic song "My Country 'Tis of Thee".

From "The Star-Spangled Banner", the US national anthem.

Exaggeration suggests he's making it up.

He sounds foolish by contradicting himself.

Could be praising them but also makes it sound like they were brainless — a little insensitive.

American slang sounds odd here — maybe he's trying to show that he understands ordinary people.

A strange way to describe dead soldiers.

Simile suggests that death is unavoidable.

Rhetorical question to finish with.

Could suggest he's nervous or that he has even more garbled words to say.

next to of course god america i

"next to of course god america i
love you land of the pilgrims' and so forth oh
say can you see by the dawn's early my
country 'tis of centuries come and go
5   and are no more what of it we should worry
in every language even deafanddumb
thy sons acclaim your glorious name by gorry
by jingo by gee by gosh by gum
why talk of beauty what could be more beaut-
10 iful than these heroic happy dead
who rushed like lions to the roaring slaughter
they did not stop to think they died instead
then shall the voice of liberty be mute?"

He spoke. And drank rapidly a glass of water

POEM DICTIONARY
acclaim — praise heavily
mute — silent

next to of course god america i

Nope, that's not a typo — E E Cummings has just shunned normal punctuation and capitalisation rules. You can do that when you're a famous poet. People often write his name as ee cummings, too.

You've Got to Know What the Poem's About

1) The poem is mocking an American <u>patriotic</u>, <u>pro-war</u> speech.
2) The last line makes it clear that the rest of the poem is spoken by a <u>character</u>, rather than reflecting the poet's <u>own opinions</u>.

A patriotic person is someone who loves their country.

Learn About the Form, Structure and Language

1) <u>FORM</u> — The first 13 lines are a <u>first-person dramatic monologue</u>. The final line is in the <u>third person</u>, describing the person giving the <u>speech</u>. The poem is a <u>parody</u> of a political speech — the form seems <u>serious</u> but the content is <u>ironic</u> and a bit <u>tongue-in-cheek</u>.

2) <u>STRUCTURE</u> — The first 13 lines are all within <u>speech marks</u>, which shows it's a <u>monologue</u> — the poet doesn't use full sentences and uses very little <u>punctuation</u>, making the phrases sound confusing and meaningless.

3) <u>PATRIOTIC LANGUAGE</u> — The poem sounds <u>inspiring</u>, but only in an <u>ironic</u> way. It's an <u>anti-war</u> poem that makes fun of patriots. It's full of <u>clichés</u>, lines from patriotic <u>songs</u> and over-the-top American <u>slang</u>.

4) <u>RHETORICAL LANGUAGE</u> — The speaker uses <u>exaggeration</u> to make his points strongly.

'Parody' is just a fancy word for 'spoof' — it's a piece of work that pokes fun at another by copying its style and saying things that sound ridiculous.

Remember the Feelings and Attitudes in the Poem

1) <u>SARCASM</u> — The poet seems to be <u>mocking</u> the speaker.
2) <u>CHALLENGING PATRIOTISM</u> — The poem challenges the popular idea of patriotism as something to be <u>proud</u> of by making the speaker use ridiculous <u>clichés</u>.
3) <u>ANTI-WAR SENTIMENTS</u> — The poem also raises serious issues about <u>death</u> in war, the <u>sincerity</u> of politicians and leaders, and whether we are too <u>gullible</u>.

Well, that's one way of showing patriotism.

Go a Step Further and give a Personal Response

Have a go at <u>answering</u> these <u>questions</u> to help you come up with <u>your own ideas</u> about the poem:

Q1.   What do you think the poet wants the public to do?
Q2.   Do you think that the ideas in this poem are still relevant today?
Q3.   Why do you think the poet has included extracts from such well-known patriotic songs?

Themes — causes of conflict, patriotism...

You should compare this poem with other poems about the same themes: causes of conflict: 'Hawk Roosting', 'The Yellow Palm', 'The Right Word'; patriotism: 'The Charge of the Light Brigade', 'Flag'.

Ted Hughes

<u>Ted Hughes</u> (1930-1998) served as the British Poet Laureate, for which he received the Order of Merit from Queen Elizabeth II, from 1984 until he died. Born in West Yorkshire, he studied at Pembroke College, Cambridge, later spending most of his life in Devon.

Hawk Roosting

It's high up in a tree and high up in the food chain.

The hawk has no time for daydreaming.

Repetition reminds us of the hawk's dangerous weapons.

I sit in the top of the wood, my eyes closed.
Inaction, no falsifying dream
Between my hooked head and hooked feet:
Or in sleep rehearse perfect kills and eat.

5   The convenience of the high trees!
The air's buoyancy and the sun's ray
Are of advantage to me;
And the earth's face upward for my inspection.

Personification of the earth as a person looking up to the hawk for approval.

The hawk imagines itself to be the only important being.

My feet are locked upon the rough bark.
10 It took the whole of Creation
To produce my foot, my each feather:
Now I hold Creation in my foot

The hawk sounds arrogant and imagines it's making the earth turn.

Or fly up, and revolve it all slowly –
I kill where I please because it is all mine.
15 There is no sophistry in my body:
My manners are tearing off heads –

The hawk has the power to decide who dies.

The hawk feels no need to explain why it feels that it is so powerful.

Violent images of the hawk attacking its prey.

The allotment of death.
For the one path of my flight is direct
Through the bones of the living.
20 No arguments assert my right:

Suggests that the hawk is in front of the sun and that the sun is supporting the hawk as well.

The hawk likes to feel it's in total control.

The sun is behind me.
Nothing has changed since I began.
My eye has permitted no change.
I am going to keep things like this.

POEM DICTIONARY
buoyancy — power to float
sophistry — reasoning that sounds clever and true but is wrong
allotment — choosing or sharing out
assert — show something is true

Hawk Roosting

If you're a fan of wildlife, you've come to the right page — this poem's all about a hawk.

You've Got to Know What the Poem's About

1) The poem is about a <u>hawk boasting</u> about its power. The hawk thinks that it is the most <u>important</u> and <u>powerful</u> creature in the world and that it <u>controls</u> the universe.

2) The hawk describes how it likes to <u>kill</u> its prey in a <u>violent</u> way.

3) It could be a <u>metaphor</u> for the behaviour of <u>political leaders</u> or <u>people</u> in general.

Learn About the Form, Structure and Language

1) <u>FORM</u> — The poem is a <u>dramatic monologue</u>, which makes the hawk's argument more direct.

2) <u>STRUCTURE</u> — The monologue ends with a <u>confident</u> statement about the <u>future</u> — showing the hawk's sense of <u>power</u> and <u>control</u>. <u>Repetition</u> makes the hawk's opinion very clear.

3) <u>FORMAL LANGUAGE</u> — The <u>arrogant</u> tone suggests that the hawk thinks it's <u>better</u> than other things.

4) <u>PERSONIFICATION</u> — The earth is personified as being <u>inferior</u> to the hawk.

5) <u>SELF-CENTRED LANGUAGE</u> — The hawk <u>talks about itself</u> a lot. This underlines how <u>central</u> and <u>important</u> it feels it is in the world.

6) <u>VIOLENT LANGUAGE</u> — The poem contains strong images of <u>violence</u> and <u>death</u>. This emphasises how brutal the hawk is.

Remember the Feelings and Attitudes in the Poem

"I'm the king of the castle..."

1) <u>POWER</u> — The poet presents the hawk as powerful and <u>destructive</u>. It's proud of its own <u>perfection</u> and power.

2) <u>ARROGANCE</u> — The hawk's attitude is <u>self-centred</u> and arrogant — it sees itself as some kind of god.

Go a Step Further and give a Personal Response

Have a go at <u>answering</u> these <u>questions</u> to help you come up with <u>your own ideas</u> about the poem:

Q1. How does the poet create a sense of the hawk's importance?

Q2. Do you think the reader is supposed to agree with the hawk's opinion of itself? What clues are there in the poem?

Q3. Why do you think the poet has chosen to write the poem in the first person?

Themes — causes of conflict, nature, death...

You should compare this poem with other poems about the same themes: causes of conflict: 'The Yellow Palm', 'The Right Word'; nature: 'The Falling Leaves'; death: 'Mametz Wood'.

John Agard

John Agard was born in Guyana in South America in 1949 and moved to Britain in 1977. He likes to perform his poems, and believes humour is an effective way of challenging people's opinions.

Flag

> What's that fluttering in a breeze?
> It's just a piece of cloth
> that brings a nation to its knees.
>
> What's that unfurling from a pole?
> 5 It's just a piece of cloth
> that makes the guts of men grow bold.
>
> What's that rising over a tent?
> It's just a piece of cloth
> that dares the coward to relent.
>
> 10 What's that flying across a field?
> It's just a piece of cloth
> that will outlive the blood you bleed.
>
> How can I possess such a cloth?
> Just ask for a flag, my friend.
> 15 Then blind your conscience to the end.

The flag could be anywhere — this shows how powerful it is.

Repetition reminds us that there is no reason for a flag to have this power.

Countries respect their flags but can be weakened by them too.

The verbs become more dramatic towards the end of the poem.

This has a double meaning — could mean bravery or battlefield injuries.

The flag of a country inspires men to fight even though they are afraid.

Enjambment (the sentence running onto the next line) puts the focus on "cloth".

Alliteration emphasises the violence of war and death.

It's as if the flag is alive and doesn't care how many lives are lost for it.

The questioner already respects the flag and wants to use its power.

These instructions sound easy, showing what a simple thing a flag actually is.

Suggests you have to ignore your morals to be patriotic.

The "piece of cloth" is just a flag.

The last two lines rhyme, which creates a neat ending.

POEM DICTIONARY
unfurling — unrolling or unfolding

Flag

Flags are more than just pretty-coloured sheets on poles. Or are they...

You've Got to Know What the Poem's About

1) The poem is about the power of a <u>national flag</u>. It's presented as a <u>conversation</u> between two characters.

2) One character asks questions about the flag, and the other character responds, explaining that the flag has the power to make people <u>fight wars</u> and <u>die</u>.

Learn About the Form, Structure and Language

1) <u>FORM</u> — The second line in each stanza is the shortest, creating a <u>blunt</u> and slightly <u>cynical</u> (mocking) tone. The <u>rhyme scheme</u> links the <u>questions</u> with the <u>answers</u> and makes the last word in each stanza <u>significant</u>.

2) <u>STRUCTURE</u> — In each stanza, the questioner asks about a <u>flag</u> and the voice answering explains the <u>powers</u> a flag can have over people. The final stanza is slightly different — the question changes, and the final answer is the most <u>cynical</u>.

3) <u>REPETITION</u> — The <u>question</u> at the start of the first four stanzas has the same <u>sentence structure</u>. Describing the flag doing different things (fluttering, unfurling etc.) suggests it can be seen in many places.

4) <u>RHETORICAL LANGUAGE</u> — Powerful commands and sarcastic language <u>engage</u> the reader.

What's that fluttering in a breeze...

Remember the Feelings and Attitudes in the Poem

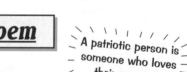

A patriotic person is someone who loves their country.

1) <u>CYNICISM</u> — The poet mocks the way people will allow a flag to have such <u>power</u> over them and to inspire whole countries to go to war.

2) <u>CONTEMPT</u> — The poet criticises the way patriotic people <u>ignore</u> their sense of <u>right and wrong</u>.

3) <u>WARNING</u> — The poem warns us about letting ourselves be <u>manipulated</u> by empty symbols.

Go a Step Further and give a Personal Response

Have a go at <u>answering</u> these <u>questions</u> to help you come up with <u>your own ideas</u> about the poem:

Q1. What kind of image of the flag does the poet present? How does he do this?

Q2. Why do you think the questioner wants to know how they can "possess such a cloth"?

Q3. Do you agree with the poet's attitude towards the flag?

Themes — causes of conflict and patriotism...

You should compare this poem with other poems about the same themes: causes of conflict: 'The Yellow Palm'; patriotism: 'Charge of the Light Brigade', 'next to of course god america i'.

Simon Armitage

Simon Armitage was born in 1963 in West Yorkshire. As well as poetry, he's also written four stage plays, and writes for TV, film and radio. He now teaches creative writing at Manchester Metropolitan University.

Extract from **Out of the Blue**

The reader is watching the TV coverage of the disaster.

Sounds vague — alliteration emphasises the distance from the people watching.

You have picked me out.
Through a distant shot of a building burning
you have noticed now
that a white cotton shirt is twirling, turning.

Gentle, calm movements are misleading at first.

Repetition emphasises repeated movement.

5   In fact I am waving, waving.
Small in the clouds, but waving, waving.
Does anyone see
a soul worth saving?

He is still expecting someone to help. He doesn't sound desperate yet.

Suggests he feels people are able to help but don't want to.

So when will you come?
10 Do you think you are watching, watching
a man shaking crumbs
or pegging out washing?

Repetition reminds us that nobody is trying to save him.

Ordinary actions contrast with the serious situation.

I am trying and trying.
The heat behind me is bullying, driving,
15 but the white of surrender is not yet flying.
I am not at the point of leaving, diving.

Reminds the reader that he has been waving a shirt.

Energetic words contrast with the gentle movement of him waving.

Usually a peaceful image, but here it shows that he's very high up.

A bird goes by.
The depth is appalling. Appalling
that others like me
20 should be wind-milling, wheeling, spiralling, falling.

Strong images of out-of-control movement.

Are your eyes believing,
believing
that here in the gills
I am still breathing.

Suggests a fish gasping for air.

25 But tiring, tiring.
Sirens below are wailing, firing.
My arm is numb and my nerves are sagging.
Do you see me, my love. I am failing, flagging.

Onomatopoeia shows the noise of the emergency vehicles but also suggests despair.

He was previously waving a flag for help, but now he's losing the will to go on.

Reminds us that he's a real person with people who care about him.

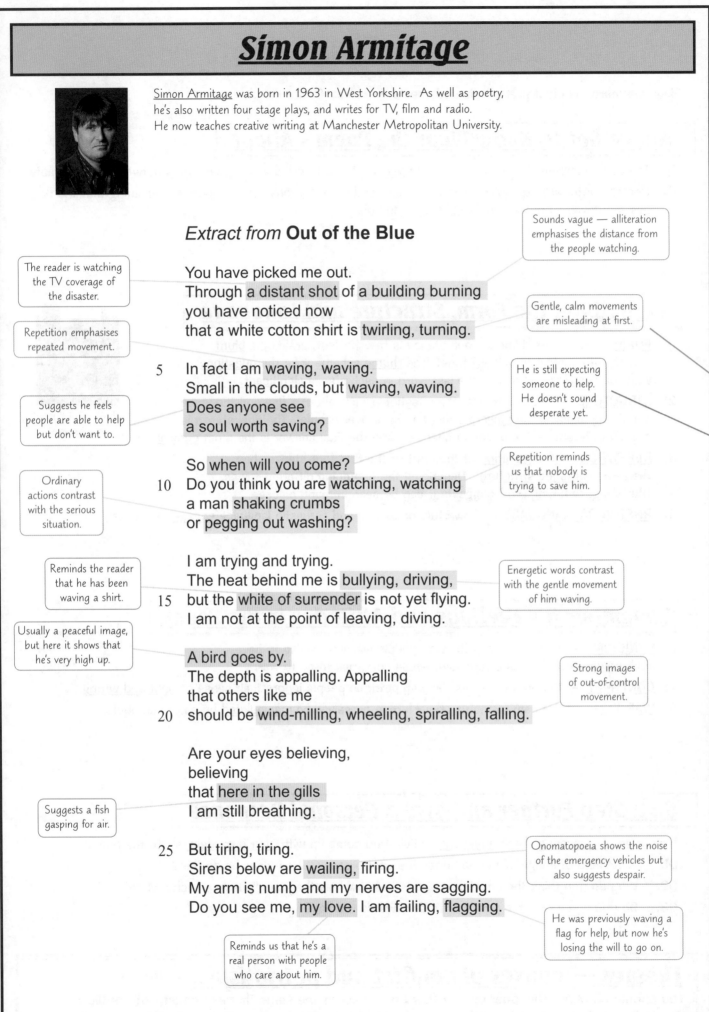

Out of the Blue

This is an extract from a long poem called "Out of the Blue" that Armitage wrote in 2006 to commemorate the September 11th terrorist attacks.

You've Got to Know What the Poem's About

1) The poem is narrated by a victim of the terrorist attacks on the <u>World Trade Centre</u> in New York in 2001.

2) He describes being in one of the <u>burning buildings</u>. He's talking to someone watching the scene on <u>TV</u>.

3) He pleads for <u>help</u>, but it's useless — the only possible outcome is <u>death</u>.

Learn About the Form, Structure and Language

1) <u>FORM</u> — The form is similar to an <u>elegy</u> — a <u>sad</u> poem about someone who has died. There is no regular <u>rhythm</u>, but the poem is full of <u>rhymes</u> and half-rhymes. This creates a sad and <u>helpless</u> tone.

2) <u>STRUCTURE</u> — In the <u>final four</u> stanzas the voice is more <u>urgent</u> as the danger gets closer and the speaker's hope of being rescued <u>fades</u>. He becomes more <u>desperate</u> toward the end of the poem.

3) <u>VERBS</u> — Verbs in the <u>present continuous</u> tense using "-ing" give us the feeling that the tragedy is happening as we are watching. It makes us feel as <u>helpless</u> as the victim.

4) <u>QUESTIONS</u> — The questions make it seem like the narrator is asking for <u>help</u> and <u>can't understand</u> why he is not being rescued.

Remember the Feelings and Attitudes in the Poem

1) <u>DESPAIR</u> — There is a sense of despair as the narrator gets <u>tired</u> of calling for help and the fire gets <u>closer</u>.

2) <u>HORROR</u> — The narrator is <u>horrified</u> at the situation as other victims <u>jump</u> from the building.

3) <u>INSIGNIFICANCE</u> — The narrator is very <u>insignificant</u> and too small to be noticed in the <u>huge scale</u> of the tragedy.

Go a Step Further and give a Personal Response

Have a go at <u>answering</u> these <u>questions</u> to help you come up with <u>your own ideas</u> about the poem:

Q1. Why is it significant that the narrator is waving a white shirt? How does the poet use this image?

Q2. Do you feel sympathy for the narrator? Why / Why not?
What other emotional reactions do you feel?

Q3. What effect does the narrator addressing the reader directly have on you?

Themes — individual experiences, helplessness and death...

You should compare this poem with other poems about the same themes: individual experiences: 'Poppies'; helplessness: 'Belfast Confetti', 'Futility'; death: 'Mametz Wood', 'Come On, Come Back'.

Owen Sheers

Owen Sheers was born in 1974 in Fiji but grew up in Abergavenny in South Wales. As well as poetry, he has worked in theatre and television, and was Writer in Residence for The Wordsworth Trust in 2004.

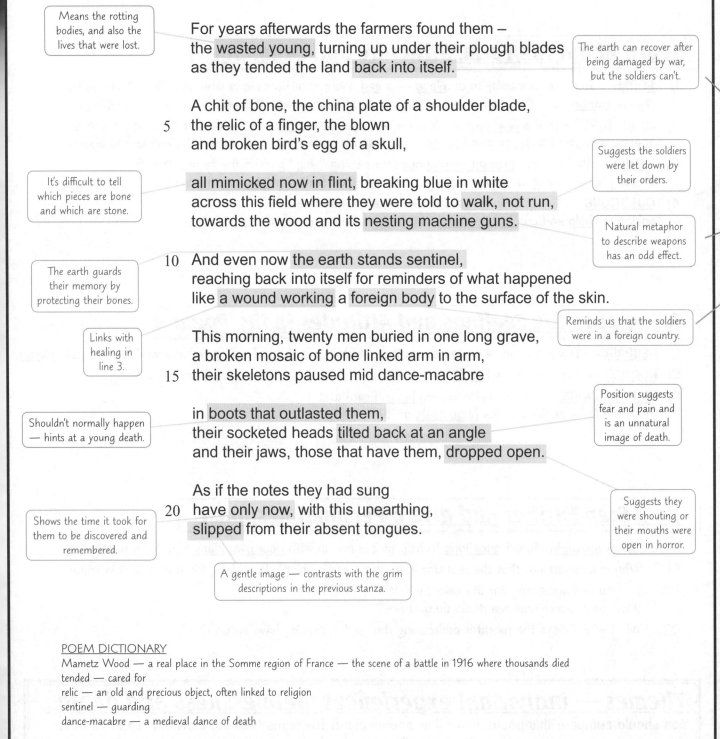

Mametz Wood

Means the rotting bodies, and also the lives that were lost.

For years afterwards the farmers found them –
the wasted young, turning up under their plough blades
as they tended the land back into itself.

The earth can recover after being damaged by war, but the soldiers can't.

A chit of bone, the china plate of a shoulder blade,
5   the relic of a finger, the blown
and broken bird's egg of a skull,

Suggests the soldiers were let down by their orders.

It's difficult to tell which pieces are bone and which are stone.

all mimicked now in flint, breaking blue in white
across this field where they were told to walk, not run,
towards the wood and its nesting machine guns.

Natural metaphor to describe weapons has an odd effect.

The earth guards their memory by protecting their bones.

10   And even now the earth stands sentinel,
reaching back into itself for reminders of what happened
like a wound working a foreign body to the surface of the skin.

Reminds us that the soldiers were in a foreign country.

Links with healing in line 3.

This morning, twenty men buried in one long grave,
a broken mosaic of bone linked arm in arm,
15   their skeletons paused mid dance-macabre

Position suggests fear and pain and is an unnatural image of death.

Shouldn't normally happen — hints at a young death.

in boots that outlasted them,
their socketed heads tilted back at an angle
and their jaws, those that have them, dropped open.

Suggests they were shouting or their mouths were open in horror.

As if the notes they had sung
20   have only now, with this unearthing,
slipped from their absent tongues.

Shows the time it took for them to be discovered and remembered.

A gentle image — contrasts with the grim descriptions in the previous stanza.

POEM DICTIONARY
Mametz Wood — a real place in the Somme region of France — the scene of a battle in 1916 where thousands died
tended — cared for
relic — an old and precious object, often linked to religion
sentinel — guarding
dance-macabre — a medieval dance of death

Mametz Wood

If you go down to Mametz Wood today, you might find something quite unpleasant...

You've Got to Know What the Poem's About

1) The poem is about <u>farmers</u> in France in the present finding <u>bones</u> and <u>skeletons</u> in their fields when they plough the land.

2) The skeletons are from <u>soldiers</u> who died during the <u>First World War</u>. The poem describes both their <u>death</u> in battle and the <u>discovery</u> of their bones in the present.

Learn About the Form, Structure and Language

1) <u>FORM</u> — The poem is written in <u>tercets</u> (3-line stanzas). It's written in the <u>third person</u>, which makes the poem feel <u>distant</u>. Long sentences and enjambment give a reflective, <u>sad</u> tone.

2) <u>STRUCTURE</u> — The poem's events are described <u>chronologically</u> (in the order they happened). The thoughtful tone and pace <u>don't change</u> and there are images of the <u>past</u> throughout the poem.

3) <u>PERSONIFICATION</u> — The <u>earth</u> is personified as someone who needs <u>healing</u> and as someone guarding the soldiers' <u>memory</u>.

> Personification is when things are described as if they're human.

4) <u>IMAGERY</u> — The poem contains lots of <u>similes</u> and <u>metaphors</u> to create clear images of the <u>farmland</u> and the <u>war</u>.

5) <u>PAST AND PRESENT</u> — Images of <u>archaeology</u> are mixed with <u>natural</u> images of the <u>present</u> to show how the bodies of the soldiers have become absorbed into the land.

Remember the Feelings and Attitudes in the Poem

1) <u>SADNESS</u> — The tone suggests a <u>calm sadness</u> for the deaths of the young soldiers.

2) <u>HORROR</u> — The horror of their death feels <u>distant</u> but is <u>suggested</u> by small details — even the <u>gory</u> images of the skeletons are described in a <u>gentle</u> tone.

3) <u>MEMORY</u> — The poem contains images of <u>nature</u> making sure that the dead soldiers are <u>remembered</u>. There's a strong sense that <u>memory</u> is important and the <u>past</u> shouldn't be forgotten.

Go a Step Further and give a Personal Response

Have a go at <u>answering</u> these <u>questions</u> to help you come up with <u>your own ideas</u> about the poem:

Q1. The poet's tone seems very detached. What clues can you see to the poet's emotions?

Q2. How does the poet create a strong impression of a rural landscape?

Themes — reality of battles, nature and death...

You should compare this poem with other poems about the same themes: reality of battles: 'Charge of the Light Brigade', 'Bayonet Charge'; nature: 'The Falling Leaves'; death: 'Out of the Blue'.

Robert Minhinnick

<u>Robert Minhinnick</u> is a Welsh poet and author, born in Neath in 1952. He studied at the University of Wales, and has won numerous awards for both his poetry and novels. He helped to establish two Welsh environmental charities and is an environmental campaigner.

The Yellow Palm

As I made my way down Palestine Street
I watched a funeral pass –
all the women waving lilac stems
around a coffin made of glass
5 and the face of the man who lay within
who had breathed a poison gas.

As I made my way down Palestine Street
I heard the call to prayer
and I stopped at the door of the golden mosque
10 to watch the faithful there
but there was blood on the walls and the muezzin's eyes
were wild with his despair.

As I made my way down Palestine Street
I met two blind beggars
15 And into their hands I pressed my hands
with a hundred black dinars;
and their salutes were those of the Imperial Guard
in the Mother of all Wars.

As I made my way down Palestine Street
20 I smelled the wide Tigris,
the river smell that lifts the air
in a city such as this;
but down on my head fell the barbarian sun
that knows no armistice.

25 As I made my way down Palestine Street
I saw a Cruise missile,
a slow and silver caravan
on its slow and silver mile,
and a beggar child turned up his face
30 and blessed it with a smile.

As I made my way down Palestine Street
under the yellow palms
I saw their branches hung with yellow dates
all sweeter than salaams,
35 and when that same child reached up to touch,
the fruit fell in his arms.

Annotations:

Sense of sight.

Repetition of this phrase separates the narrator from everything going on in the street.

Sounds like a fairy tale — makes the last line of the stanza more of a shock.

Sense of hearing.

He still sounds detached.

Contrasts with the beauty of the mosque and links religion and violence.

Sense of touch shows his connection with the people he sees.

Saddam Hussein used this expression about the First Gulf War (1990-1991).

Links the beggars to a more violent past.

Sense of smell makes the river sound alive.

Suggestion of war links with next stanza.

Personifies the sun as ruthless — even nature can be in conflict.

Repetition emphasises beauty and grace, even though it's a weapon.

Makes the child sound innocent and fragile.

The child seems like a holy figure, maybe because he's not at fault for the war.

Alliteration emphasises positive words and introduces the sense of taste.

<u>POEM DICTIONARY</u>
Palestine Street — a street in the centre of Baghdad
muezzin — someone who calls people to prayer in a mosque
Imperial Guard — troops who guarded Saddam Hussein
Tigris — the river that runs through Baghdad
armistice — when enemies agree to stop fighting
salaam — Islamic greeting meaning 'peace'

The Yellow Palm

This poem's not a great advert for going on holiday to Baghdad — I think I'll stick to Tenerife.

You've Got to Know What the Poem's About

1) The poem describes what the narrator sees as he walks along a main street in Baghdad.
2) The narrator sees both violent and peaceful scenes as he walks along the street.

Learn About the Form, Structure and Language

1) FORM — The poem is written in the first person. The 2nd, 4th and last lines in each stanza rhyme. The last two lines of each stanza introduce new details that challenge the images in the previous four lines.
2) STRUCTURE — Each stanza is linked to the next through small details. This supports the idea of a long street full of different but related things.
3) REPETITION — Repeating the first line in each stanza shows the narrator's movement along the street.
4) VIVID DESCRIPTION — There is a lot of strong imagery and description in the poem. The range of colours makes the description vivid.
5) SENSES — A range of first-person verbs shows the narrator using all his senses — this makes the street feel busy.

Remember the Feelings and Attitudes in the Poem

1) SUGGESTED CRITICISM — The narrator doesn't give his opinions but leaves the reader to make connections between the details of the poem and political ideas. The poem suggests that human behaviour is violent and harmful.
2) CONFUSION — The narrator finds contradictions between the positive things he sees and the violence and pain that human society has caused.
3) DETACHMENT — The narrator seems to step back, as though he's presenting us with evidence and letting us draw our own conclusions.

Go a Step Further and give a Personal Response

Have a go at answering these questions to help you come up with your own ideas about the poem:

Q1.   The poem is set in Iraq. How is it relevant to other parts of the world?

Q2.   Why do you think the poet has made the final stanza the only one without any negative details in it?

Q3.   What sort of attitude does the character in the poem have towards what he sees?

Themes — causes of conflict and divided society...

You should compare this poem with other poems about the same themes: causes of conflict: 'Hawk Roosting', 'next to of course god america i'; division: 'The Right Word', 'At the Border, 1979'.

Imtiaz Dharker

Imtiaz Dharker was born in 1954 in Pakistan. She has said that she believes identity comes from "beliefs and states of mind", rather than nationality or religion.

The Right Word

Outside the door,
lurking in the shadows,
is a terrorist.

Is that the wrong description?
5   Outside that door,
taking shelter in the shadows,
is a freedom-fighter.

I haven't got this right.
Outside, waiting in the shadows,
10   is a hostile militant.

Are words no more
than waving, wavering flags?
Outside your door,
watchful in the shadows,
15   is a guerrilla warrior.

God help me.
Outside, defying every shadow,
stands a martyr.
I saw his face.

20   No words can help me now.
Just outside the door,
lost in shadows,
is a child who looks like mine.

One word for you.
25   Outside my door,
his hand too steady,
his eyes too hard
is a boy who looks like your son, too.

I open the door.
30   Come in, I say.
Come in and eat with us.

The child steps in
and carefully, at my door,
takes off his shoes.

Two different words for the same action, but one sounds threatening and the other sounds vulnerable.

This noun is straight to the point and sets a frightening tone for the poem.

Shows how difficult it is to agree on right and wrong.

Ironic tone suggests there's no right or wrong answer.

A much more positive description than in the first stanza.

Repeated image of shadows suggests confusion and fear.

Suggests patriotism as well as poor communication.

Another threatening term suggesting power and violence.

Scary idea of someone willing to die and kill for their religious beliefs.

Speaker has become more and more helpless.

The activist is just as uncertain as the speaker.

Shows that the activist isn't that different from the narrator.

The speaker has given up on finding the right term and wants to talk clearly.

Challenges reader to think about the situation personally.

Repetition shows he is welcome.

A welcoming activity, suggesting friendship and sharing.

After all the threatening descriptions, this may be "the right word".

The child is gentle and thoughtful — this shows how things could be.

POEM DICTIONARY
wavering — hesitating from making a decision
guerrilla — a type of warfare involving small groups of soldiers with limited training and equipment
martyr — someone who sacrifices their life for their beliefs

The Right Word

Sometimes it can be hard to find the right, erm, you know, the right whatsit...

You've Got to Know What the Poem's About

1) The poem is about a <u>suspicious</u> and <u>divided</u> community, where different viewpoints lead to <u>violence</u>.
2) The narrator tries to find an accurate way to describe a <u>young stranger</u> who at first seems threatening.
3) At the end, the stranger seems to be just a <u>harmless child</u>.

Learn About the Form, Structure and Language

1) <u>FORM</u> — The poem is written in the <u>first person</u>, making it seem personal. The stanzas have no regular rhythm or rhyme and are of different lengths — this shows the uncertainty of the situation.
2) <u>STRUCTURE</u> — Each of the first seven stanzas is a separate way of <u>describing</u> the young man. Stanzas 1 to 3 are an <u>ironic</u> 'search' for the correct words, stanzas 4 to 6 suggest that it is <u>too hard</u> to find the right words, and stanzas 7 to 9 describe the real <u>truth</u> of the situation.
3) <u>REPETITION</u> — Phrases are <u>repeated</u> with small <u>changes</u>, as if the speaker keeps trying to correct herself. Repeating words like "door" and "shadows" suggest <u>barriers</u> and <u>suspicion</u> between people.
4) <u>EMOTIVE LANGUAGE</u> — The poet uses lots of <u>emotive</u> words to describe activists and their actions.
5) <u>CONVERSATIONAL STYLE</u> — The narrator speaks directly to the reader. The poet uses <u>questions</u> to show that the speaker is <u>struggling</u> to know which words to use.

Remember the Feelings and Attitudes in the Poem

1) <u>IMPORTANCE OF LANGUAGE</u> — The poem suggests that language is <u>important</u>, and that words can influence people's <u>attitudes</u> and create <u>fear</u> and <u>suspicion</u>.
2) <u>ANXIETY</u> — The descriptions of the stranger in the first five stanzas show how <u>afraid</u> and <u>suspicious</u> people can be.
3) <u>DESIRE FOR FRIENDSHIP</u> — There is a sense of <u>understanding</u> at the end when the speaker <u>sees past</u> their <u>first impressions</u> of the stranger.

Mabel was knitting a hat. No, hang on, Mabel was knitting a head-warming device...

Go a Step Further and give a Personal Response

Have a go at <u>answering</u> these <u>questions</u> to help you come up with <u>your own ideas</u> about the poem:

Q1. What does the poem's title mean?
Q2. Does language create barriers amongst people in your own society?
Q3. What does this poem suggest to you about the media and the general public?

Themes — causes of conflict and divided society...

You should compare this poem with other poems about the same themes: causes of conflict: 'The Yellow Palm', 'next to of course god america i'; divided society: 'At the Border, 1979'.

Choman Hardi

Choman Hardi was born in 1974 in Iraqi Kurdistan, but spent from 1975 to 1979 with her family in Iran. In 1993 she arrived in the UK as a refugee, and went on to study at Oxford, London and Kent Universities. She has published poetry in both Kurdish and English.

At the Border, 1979

Suggests control by officials.

They expect everything to be different when they're in a different country.

'It is your last check-in point in this country!'
We grabbed a drink –
soon everything would taste different.

A man-made division.

5 The land under our feet continued
divided by a thick iron chain.

It's easy to physically cross the border.

My sister put her leg across it.
'Look over here,' she said to us,
'my right leg is in this country
and my left leg in the other.'
10 The border guards told her off.

This makes the guards seem silly for caring about something so petty.

Caesura (a pause in the middle of a line) makes the mother's words seem grand and important.

The mother's patriotism makes her exaggerate.

My mother informed me: *We are going home.*
She said that the roads are much cleaner
the landscape is more beautiful
and people are much kinder.

The adults' reaction seems dramatic.

15 Dozens of families waited in the rain.
'I can inhale home,' somebody said.
Now our mothers were crying. I was five years old
standing by the check-in point
comparing both sides of the border.

The only differences between the countries are man-made.

Sounds calm and logical compared to the adults' behaviour.

20 The autumn soil continued on the other side
with the same colour, the same texture.
It rained on both sides of the chain.

Repetition for emphasis.

Simple statement of fact — unlike the adults, she's unaffected by emotions.

We waited while our papers were checked,
our faces thoroughly inspected.
25 Then the chain was removed to let us through.
A man bent down and kissed his muddy homeland.
The same chain of mountains encompassed all of us.

The controllers sound powerful and unfriendly.

Makes his reaction seem over the top, as the land is nothing special.

Contrasts with the earlier image of "chain" — this is a natural boundary holding different people together.

POEM DICTIONARY
encompassed — surrounded or enclosed

At the Border, 1979

Crossing a border can be quite emotional. Especially if you trip over it.

You've Got to Know What the Poem's About

1) The poem is about a child crossing a <u>border</u> back into their <u>homeland</u>. The family sound <u>helpless</u> and worried.

2) The <u>adults</u> become very <u>emotional</u> about crossing the border. The narrator <u>can't understand</u> why it's so important to them when things look <u>the same</u> on both sides of the border.

They're a cheery lot, those border guards...

Learn About the Form, Structure and Language

1) <u>FORM</u> — The poem is written in the <u>first person</u>, showing it's a personal memory. The stanzas are different lengths, suggesting that the narrator is describing the scene by piecing together <u>smaller memories</u>.

2) <u>STRUCTURE</u> — The poem starts with lots of <u>direct speech</u>. The tone becomes more <u>thoughtful</u> towards the end as the poet describes how both sides of the border are the same.

3) <u>CHILD-LIKE LANGUAGE</u> — The poem is written in a <u>simple</u>, <u>chatty</u> style with no fancy descriptions or imagery. The short sentences sound child-like and make the poet's feelings about borders seem <u>obvious</u>.

4) <u>DIRECT SPEECH</u> — Natural conversation makes the scene more <u>convincing</u> and <u>real</u>.

5) <u>PASSIVE SENTENCES</u> — Impersonal descriptions show how the families are in the power of the <u>officials</u> who decide on national boundaries.

Remember the Feelings and Attitudes in the Poem

1) <u>NATIONALISM</u> — There's a sense that people have their feelings and attitudes <u>controlled</u> by nationalism, and that national boundaries and restrictions have <u>negative</u> effects.

2) <u>CHILD-LIKE VIEW</u> — There's a contrast between the child's <u>logical</u> point of view and the more <u>complex</u> emotions of adults.

Nationalists are proud of their country and can be prejudiced, sometimes thinking that their nation is automatically better than other countries.

Go a Step Further and give a Personal Response

Have a go at <u>answering</u> these <u>questions</u> to help you come up with <u>your own ideas</u> about the poem:

Q1. Whose attitude do you agree with most, the adults' or the children's? Why?

Q2. Does the poem give you any ideas about why their homeland is so important to the families?

Q3. What examples of humour can you find in the poem? What effect do they have?

Themes — divided society and helplessness...

You should compare this poem with other poems about the same themes: divided society: 'The Right Word', 'Belfast Confetti', 'The Yellow Palm'; helplessness: 'Out of the Blue', 'Futility'.

Ciaran Carson

Ciaran Carson was born in Belfast in 1948. After graduating from Queen's University in Belfast he worked for the Arts Council of Northern Ireland. He became a Professor at Queen's University in 1998, as well as being Director of the Seamus Heaney Centre for Poetry.

Riots were sometimes started to lure the security services to the scene of a bomb.

An image of celebration is used ironically to describe shrapnel from IRA bombs.

Metaphor gives visual image of explosion.

Belfast Confetti

Suddenly as the riot squad moved in it was raining exclamation marks,
Nuts, bolts, nails, car-keys. A fount of broken type. And the explosion
5 Itself – an asterisk on the map. This hyphenated line, a burst of rapid fire...
I was trying to complete a sentence in my head, but it kept stuttering,
All the alleyways and side streets blocked with stops and
10 colons.

I know this labyrinth so well – Balaklava, Raglan, Inkerman, Odessa Street –
Why can't I escape? Every move is punctuated. Crimea Street. Dead end again.
15 A Saracen, Kremlin-2 mesh. Makrolon face-shields. Walkie-talkies. What is
My name? Where am I coming from? Where am I going? A fusillade of question-marks.

An asterisk (*) looks like an explosion, and might be how the security forces mark it on a map.

Suggests damage as well as being unable to describe the scene.

Reflects the sound of gunfire and the speaker's fear.

He's trying to escape, but roadblocks stop him.

Shows how much trouble he's in as he's lost in an area he knows.

He keeps hesitating.

He's having these questions shouted at him.

It's as though he's being attacked by the questions.

He's surrounded by confusing communication from security forces.

POEM DICTIONARY
asterisk — this symbol ➡ *
hyphenated line — a line of dashes (-----)
labyrinth — a maze
Balaklava, Raglan, Inkerman, Odessa Street, Crimea Street — areas and roads in Belfast
Saracen — an army vehicle
Makrolon — a type of plastic
fusillade — many shots fired at the same time

Belfast Confetti

This poem's set in Northern Ireland during 'The Troubles' — a period when there were lots of terrorist incidents between Catholic nationalists and Protestant unionists.

You've Got to Know What the Poem's About

1) The narrator is caught up in a <u>bomb incident</u> in Belfast.

2) He describes his actions as he tries to get away from the bomb to <u>safety</u>. Every time he tries to escape, he is <u>stopped</u> by security forces and confusion.

Learn About the Form, Structure and Language

Debbie and Phil were hoping for just ordinary, run-of-the-mill confetti.

1) <u>FORM</u> — Uneven line lengths, incomplete sentences, ellipsis (missing text) and enjambment all give an <u>uneven</u> feel to the comments. Long lines are followed by short lines, as if the poet keeps reaching <u>dead ends</u>.

2) <u>STRUCTURE</u> — The poem seems to start in the <u>middle</u> of the event and there is no clear <u>ending</u>. The language changes from <u>past</u> to <u>present</u> tense between the first and second stanza to show that the narrator is <u>still trapped</u>.

3) <u>IMAGERY</u> — The poem contains lots of metaphors, which describe <u>violence</u> and <u>language</u> as having similar <u>damaging</u> effects. It also hints at <u>poor communication</u>.

4) <u>CHAOTIC LANGUAGE</u> — <u>Questions</u> show the <u>confusion</u> the character is feeling. There are lots of <u>lists</u> that suggest noise and <u>chaos</u>.

Remember the Feelings and Attitudes in the Poem

1) <u>BEING TRAPPED</u> — There is a feeling of being trapped by both the <u>physical blockades</u> and the <u>language</u> used by the security forces to control who goes where.

2) <u>VIOLENCE</u> — <u>Physical</u> and <u>verbal</u> violence confuse and upset the speaker.

3) <u>FEAR AND CONFUSION</u> — The poem shows a personal <u>emotional reaction</u> to a Belfast bomb incident. These were often reported in an <u>impersonal</u> way in the newspapers.

Go a Step Further and give a Personal Response

Have a go at <u>answering</u> these <u>questions</u> to help you come up with <u>your own ideas</u> about the poem:

Q1. What does the speaker suggest about himself in the poem?

Q2. Is the poem just about the Belfast troubles, or is it relevant to anywhere else in the world?

Q3. Could the poem have anything to say about the way war is reported?

Themes — reality of battles, divided society...

You should compare this poem with other poems about the same themes: reality of battles: 'The Charge of the Light Brigade', 'Bayonet Charge'; divided society: 'The Right Word', 'The Yellow Palm'.

Jane Weir

<u>Jane Weir</u> was born in Salford in 1963 but currently lives and works in Derbyshire. She spent several years in Belfast in Northern Ireland.

Poppies

Three days before Armistice Sunday
and poppies had already been placed
on individual war graves. Before you left,
I pinned one onto your lapel, crimped petals,
5   spasms of paper red, disrupting a blockade
of yellow bias binding around your blazer.

Sellotape bandaged around my hand,
I rounded up as many white cat hairs
as I could, smoothed down your shirt's
10 upturned collar, steeled the softening
of my face. I wanted to graze my nose
across the tip of your nose, play at
being Eskimos like we did when
you were little. I resisted the impulse
15 to run my fingers through the gelled
blackthorns of your hair. All my words
flattened, rolled, turned into felt,

slowly melting. I was brave, as I walked
with you, to the front door, threw
20 it open, the world overflowing
like a treasure chest. A split second
and you were away, intoxicated.
After you'd gone I went into your bedroom,
released a song bird from its cage.
25 Later a single dove flew from the pear tree,
and this is where it has led me,
skirting the church yard walls, my stomach busy
making tucks, darts, pleats, hat-less, without
a winter coat or reinforcements of scarf, gloves.

30 On reaching the top of the hill I traced
the inscriptions on the war memorial,
leaned against it like a wishbone.
The dove pulled freely against the sky,
an ornamental stitch. I listened, hoping to hear
35 your playground voice catching on the wind.

Annotations:

A creepy reminder that war kills individuals, so loss is personal.

Makes the reader think of an injured body.

She is emotionally wounded and he might be wounded in war.

Simile shows the world from the son's point of view — makes it sound exciting.

Doves are a symbol of peace but also loss.

Sewing imagery shows she's nervous.

Image of something small and beautiful in a large space represents her son.

Repetition shows both the country and the soldiers' families feel loss.

Suggests that she feels shut out from her son's life.

Could be a school uniform as well as an army one.

She's still treating him like a child.

Alliteration shows she's trying to be brave and not show emotion.

Metaphor suggests he's no longer a child because he's styled his hair.

Sudden movement suggests breaking a barrier to freedom.

The son's excitement contrasts with his mother's sadness.

Represents her son leaving.

Battle imagery makes her sound vulnerable.

A reminder of the risks her son faces.

Links leaving to join the army with leaving to go to school.

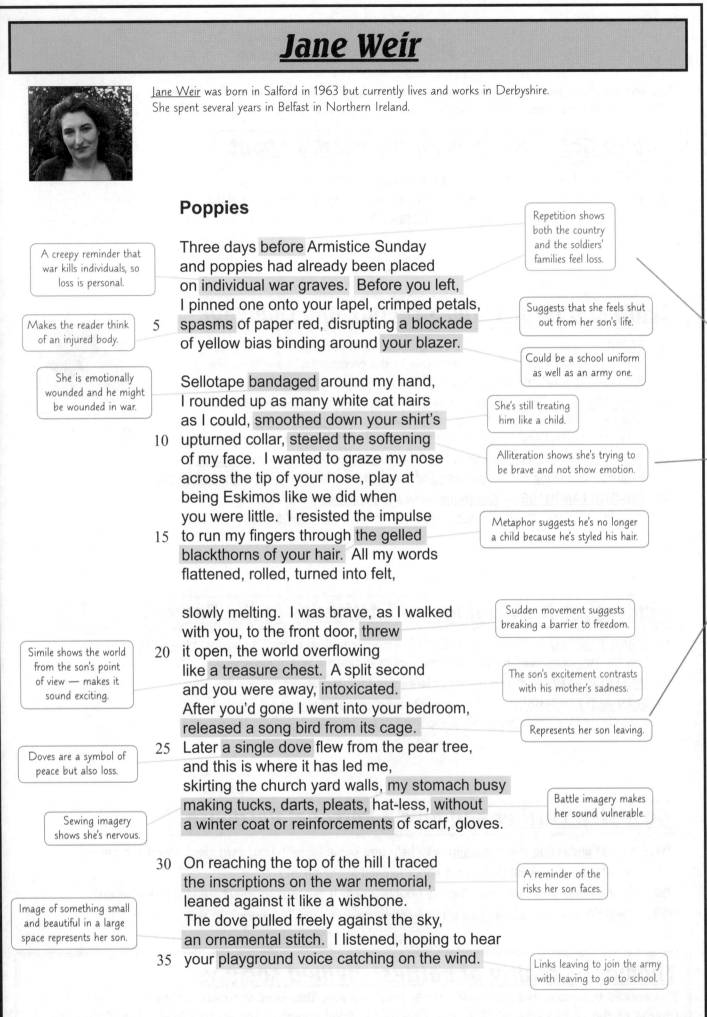

<u>*Poppies*</u>

Poppies are nice. Being a mother whose son goes off to fight in a war isn't quite so nice.

<u>*You've Got to Know What the Poem's About*</u>

1) A <u>mother</u> describes her son leaving home to fight in the <u>army</u>.
2) She feels <u>sad</u>, <u>lonely</u> and <u>scared</u> for his safety.
3) She helps him smarten his <u>uniform</u> and after he leaves, she goes to places that <u>remind</u> her of him, desperately trying to find any trace of him.

<u>*Learn About the Form, Structure and Language*</u>

1) <u>FORM</u> — There is no regular <u>rhyme</u> or <u>rhythm</u> and the poet uses <u>long sentences</u> and <u>enjambment</u>. These features make the narrator seem as though she's deep in thought.
2) <u>STRUCTURE</u> — The poem starts with her son <u>leaving</u> and then describes what she did <u>afterwards</u>. The time frame in the poem is <u>unclear</u> — many of the images could describe a child going to <u>school</u> for the first time.
3) <u>EMOTIONAL LANGUAGE</u> — There are lots of statements beginning with the <u>first person</u>, e.g. "I...". This gives us a clear idea of the mother's emotions.
4) <u>METAPHORS</u> — Images of war and <u>loss</u> are mixed with <u>household</u> imagery. <u>Birds</u> are symbols of <u>freedom</u> to describe the son leaving the safety of his home for the excitement of the wider world.

<u>*Remember the Feelings and Attitudes in the Poem*</u>

1) <u>LOSS</u> — The mother is <u>sad</u> about her son leaving.
2) <u>FEAR</u> — She is <u>afraid</u> for her son's safety. The poem focuses on the <u>bravery</u> of the families left behind when young men go to war.
3) <u>FREEDOM</u> — The poem contrasts the <u>loss</u> the mother feels with her son's feelings of <u>freedom</u> and excitement.

<u>*Go a Step Further and give a Personal Response*</u>

Have a go at <u>answering</u> these <u>questions</u> to help you come up with <u>your own ideas</u> about the poem:

Q1. Is this a poem about war or a poem about families?
Q2. What impression does the poet give you of the mother through the things that she does?
Q3. How do you think the title relates to the poem?

Themes — effects of conflict, sadness and loss...

You should compare this poem with other poems about the same themes: effects of conflict: 'The Charge of the Light Brigade'; sadness and loss: 'Futility', 'The Falling Leaves', 'Come On, Come Back'.

Conflict — Causes

Conflicts can start off as small <u>disagreements</u>, but they might end up as <u>wars</u>...

> 1) Conflict is when different people, groups or countries <u>disagree</u> with each other.
> 2) Conflict between <u>groups</u> can lead to fear and violence.
>   Conflict between <u>countries</u> can lead to wars.
> 3) There are many reasons for conflict, including <u>political</u> and <u>religious</u> differences.

Conflict can be caused by Difference

The Yellow Palm (Pages 24-25)

1) People have come to pray at the mosque but there is "<u>blood</u> on the walls" and "<u>despair</u>" in the muezzin's eyes. This suggests that <u>religion</u> can cause conflict.
2) The reference to the "<u>Imperial Guard</u>" (Saddam Hussein's bodyguards) hints at the power of a <u>cruel</u> and <u>ambitious</u> leader who could lead a country to war.

Hawk Roosting (Pages 16-17)

1) The narrator is a hawk — a natural <u>killer</u>. It believes that "the allotment of death" is its right.
2) Although the hawk is <u>confident</u>, it is <u>tricking</u> itself — it thinks that it controls the Earth.
3) <u>Pro-war politicians</u> are known as "hawks", so the poem could be describing how arrogant, <u>powerful</u> people can lead a whole country into war.

Language can encourage conflict

next to of course god america i (Pages 14-15)

1) The poet shows that <u>language</u> can be used to encourage people to get involved in conflict.
2) The speaker in the poem uses <u>persuasive language</u> to make his listeners keen to fight. Descriptions of "heroic happy dead" who "rushed like lions to the roaring slaughter" sound energetic and <u>exciting</u>, but the words "dead" and "slaughter" sound <u>threatening</u>.
3) The last line makes the speaker sound <u>awkward</u> and nervous. The poet <u>mocks</u> the way this character uses the power of language to <u>mislead</u> people.

Flag (Pages 18-19)

1) The poem shows that <u>patriotism</u> can cause people to <u>ignore</u> their <u>conscience</u> and start wars.
2) A flag is really "just a piece of cloth", but when people see it as something <u>more important</u> they are willing to <u>kill</u> and <u>die</u> for it — it "makes the guts of men grow bold".

Conflict can also be caused by telling someone they look silly in their leotard.

Other poems also feature the causes of conflict...

'The Right Word' shows how using <u>suspicious</u> and frightened <u>language</u> can cause <u>mistrust</u> and <u>fear</u> within a community, which can lead to <u>conflict</u>.

Conflict — Effects

No prizes for working out that the effects of conflict <u>aren't</u> likely to be good...

> 1) Conflict can <u>kill</u> and <u>injure</u> soldiers and civilians.
> 2) People can be <u>mentally scarred</u> by their experiences.
> 3) Even people <u>not directly involved</u> in conflict can be affected by it, e.g. the families of soldiers fighting in wars.

Conflict affects the people who Fight

Futility (Pages 4-5)

1) The poem focuses on the <u>waste</u> of human life caused by war, using a <u>single</u> soldier to describe the <u>wider effects</u> of war.
2) The narrator feels <u>angry</u> that the energy that went into creating life — "limbs, so dear-achieved" — has been wasted.

The Charge of the Light Brigade (Pages 6-7)

1) The poem focuses on the <u>number</u> of men killed in battle as the result of a single order. There are several mentions of "the six hundred", showing <u>how many</u> men there were to start with compared to how few <u>survived</u> — "Then they rode back, but not / Not the six hundred".
2) The poem shows that war can make people <u>brave</u>. The soldiers do their duty even though they know they will probably be <u>killed</u>.

Bayonet Charge (Pages 10-11)

1) The poem describes the <u>pain</u> and <u>fear</u> a <u>single soldier</u> experiences during battle. The soldier is a helpless <u>victim</u>, "running", "Stumbling" and "Sweating".
2) Fighting has also <u>destroyed</u> the <u>patriotic feelings</u> that the soldier had to begin with — "King, honour, human dignity, etcetera / Dropped like luxuries".

Conflict affects people who are Not Directly Involved in it

Poppies (Pages 32-33)

1) The poem describes the <u>pain</u> and sadness of a mother whose son is going away to <u>fight</u> in a war.
2) She feels as if she has <u>lost</u> him even before he has left — his uniform has a "blockade / of yellow bias binding" <u>keeping them apart</u>.
3) After he leaves, her constant worrying about her son's safety has a <u>physical effect</u> on her — she describes her stomach as "busy / making tucks, darts, pleats".

Other poems also feature the effects of conflict...

'Out of the Blue' shows the <u>devastating</u> effect of political conflict on one man. In 'Come On, Come Back', Vaudevue is so <u>psychologically damaged</u> by war that she <u>ends up dead</u>.

Reality of Battles

These poems explain what it's really like to be involved in conflict.

> 1) Some poems are set right in the thick of the action.
> 2) Poets can describe the sights and sounds of the battle to help us understand what it's really like to be there.

The Horror of the battle can be Described Clearly...

The Charge of the Light Brigade (Pages 6-7)

1) The chaos, noise and danger of the battle is described in detail. The men are "Storm'd at with shot and shell" and "Plunged in the battery-smoke" of the enemies' cannons.
2) The description of the battleground as "the jaws of Death" and "the mouth of Hell" shows that battle is dangerous and scary.

Bayonet Charge (Pages 10-11)

1) The poem focuses on just one soldier's thoughts and emotions during a battle.
2) The soldier's pain and fear is clear. He is running "In raw-seamed hot khaki" and "Sweating like molten iron". He is motivated by panic — "His terror's touchy dynamite".
3) The descriptions of the battle create a sense of noise and confusion. He can hear "Bullets smacking the belly out of the air" and is running through "shot-slashed furrows". We are given a clear picture of the dangers he is facing.

Belfast Confetti (Pages 30-31)

1) The poem describes an upset and confused person caught up in a conflict. The first-person voice helps us to understand the character's thoughts.
2) Metaphors for the character's confused thoughts also refer to physical danger, e.g. "a burst / of rapid fire", "A fusillade of question-marks".
3) The description of the explosion raining "Nuts, bolts, nails, car-keys" makes the bomb feel real.

> A metaphor is when something is described as being something else.

...or it can be Implied

Mametz Wood (Pages 22-23)

1) The horror of the battle is suggested by the details of what is being found many years later. The image of "a broken mosaic of bone" shows how their bodies were torn apart by fighting.
2) Metaphors like "the china plate of a shoulder blade" and "broken bird's egg of a skull" show how fragile the soldiers' skeletons were — they could be easily damaged in battle.

Other poems also feature the reality of battles...

'Futility' is about a soldier dying in France in the First World War. 'Hawk Roosting' contains descriptions of a hawk killing its prey, which could suggest killing and being killed in wars.

Nature

Natural imagery like animals, trees, fields and plants adds to the meaning of these poems.

> 1) Peaceful natural images can provide a contrast if the poem is describing something horrific like a war.
>
> 2) Natural images can also be used as a metaphor to suggest something else.

Nature can be a Major Theme in the poem

Hawk Roosting (Pages 16-17)

1) The poem describes violence in a natural setting. In this case, a natural predator is a metaphor for human violence.
2) The hawk thinks it is in control of nature — it says "I hold Creation in my foot". It sees the earth and all of nature as less important than it.

The Falling Leaves (Pages 12-13)

1) The poem compares the falling of old "brown leaves" — a natural event — with the deaths of young men in war — something that is not natural.
2) The dead leaves and soldiers are both compared to "snowflakes wiping out the noon". This makes us think of coldness, darkness and death.

Some poems have nature as the Background

Mametz Wood (Pages 22-23)

1) As well as the deaths of the soldiers, the poet describes the damage to the land where the battles took place.
2) The earth is personified as patient and watchful. It "stands sentinel", as if it's guarding the memory of the soldiers who died.

Bayonet Charge (Pages 10-11)

1) The natural setting where the battle takes place is described as if its beauty has been destroyed by human fighting.
2) The poem describes the agony of a hare wounded by the gunfire in a vivid and disturbing way. This creates a parallel between the hare's innocence and pain and that of the soldier.

Other poems also feature the theme of nature...

'Out of the Blue' uses some natural images like "here in the gills / I am still breathing" to emphasise the narrator's pain and despair. 'The Yellow Palm' includes natural elements like the river and the "barbarian sun" to create a strong impression of what Baghdad is like.

Sadness and Loss

If anything's likely to cause feelings of <u>sadness</u> and <u>loss</u>, it's conflict...

> 1) The <u>loss of life</u> in wars leads to <u>grief</u> for the friends
> and families of the people who are killed or in danger.
>
> 2) Conflict can also cause sadness and loss because of the
> <u>physical</u> and <u>mental</u> harm it causes to the people involved in it.

War Casualties cause feelings of Sadness and Loss

Futility (Pages 4-5)

1) The soldier had already lost the <u>peaceful life</u> that he had before the war.
2) The poet uses the loss of <u>one individual</u> to make us think about the <u>many</u> who have died in war.
3) The narrator shows us that human life is <u>precious</u> — "limbs, so dear-achieved" — which makes the loss of life even more sad.

The Falling Leaves (Pages 12-13)

1) The poem's <u>calm atmosphere</u> makes the feelings of sadness stronger. The leaves, representing the dead men, fall "thickly, silently", showing the huge <u>number</u> of lives lost.
2) The narrator says she "wandered slowly", which suggests she's <u>thoughtful</u> and <u>sad</u>. The <u>first-person narration</u> helps the reader understand the narrator's <u>sadness</u>.

> Writing in the first person uses words like 'I', 'me', 'my', 'we', 'us' and 'our'.

Conflict can cause Sadness and Loss in Other Ways too

'Come On, Come Back' (Pages 8-9)

1) At the start of the poem Vaudevue has already lost her <u>memory</u> because of the war — she is "as a child, an idiot, as one without memory".
2) By the end of the poem she has also lost her <u>life</u>.

Poppies (Pages 32-33)

1) The mother feels like she has lost her <u>son</u> when he leaves home to join the army.
2) She also feels like she has lost the <u>connection</u> she had with him when he was a child. When he's gone, she is "hoping to hear / your playground voice" — she feels just like she did when he <u>started school</u>.

Toby was very sad when he missed his favourite TV programme.

Other poems also feature sadness and loss...

In 'The Charge of the Light Brigade', the poet praises the soldiers who were <u>killed</u> in the battle. In 'Out of the Blue', the narrator is sad about <u>his own</u> imminent death — "Do you see me, my love. I am failing, flagging." Ahhh — there's nothing like a nice jolly poem to cheer you up...

Divided Society

These poems show how societies become <u>divided</u>, and the <u>problems</u> that this can cause.

> 1) Communities can be divided because of <u>race</u>, <u>religion</u>, <u>political beliefs</u>, etc. This creates <u>tension</u> between members of the community, which can sometimes lead to <u>violence</u>.
>
> 2) In a divided society people often feel <u>scared</u> and <u>suspicious</u> of each other.

Divisions *are caused by people's* Attitudes

The Right Word (Pages 26-27)

1) The poem suggests that the way people <u>describe</u> each other creates <u>fear</u>, which <u>separates</u> them. Words like "terrorist", "hostile militant" and "guerrilla warrior" all sound extreme and <u>dangerous</u>.
2) The narrator repeats "outside" and refers to "my door" and "your door", which suggests people <u>blocking themselves off</u> from each other.
3) Near the end of the poem the activist is described as "a child who looks like mine" and "a boy who looks like your son, too". This suggests that <u>barriers</u> have been broken.

At the Border, 1979 (Pages 28-29)

1) The poem suggests that <u>borders</u> between different countries create <u>prejudice</u>. The mother says that "the roads are much cleaner", the landscape is "more beautiful" and the people are "much kinder" in her home country.
2) The border is "a thick iron chain" that <u>divides</u> people. The narrator points out how <u>artificial</u> the border is when "The <u>same</u> chain of mountains encompassed all of us".

Divisions *can lead to* Armed Conflict

Belfast Confetti (Pages 30-31)

1) The poem suggests that <u>tension</u> between different groups has damaged the lives of <u>ordinary people</u> living in Belfast.
2) The city is described as being <u>physically divided</u> by roadblocks, reflecting how Belfast was split into Loyalist and Republican areas — "All the alleyways and side streets blocked".

The Yellow Palm (Pages 24-25)

1) The description of the city suggests a society that has been <u>broken</u> by war and violence.
2) There is a split between what things <u>should</u> be like and what is <u>actually happening</u> — the "golden mosque" has "blood on the walls".
3) Even <u>nature</u> seems <u>divided</u> — the river Tigris has a smell that "lifts the air", but the "barbarian sun" beats down ruthlessly.

Other poems also feature the theme of divided society...

'Flag' shows how flags can create a strong sense of <u>national identity</u> that encourages <u>divisions</u> with other countries, which can lead to <u>conflict</u>. The idea that extreme patriotism creates <u>divisions</u> and <u>conflict</u> with other nations is also found in 'next to of course god america i'.

Patriotism

Patriotism can be a <u>good</u> thing, but it can also cause an awful lot of <u>problems</u>...

> 1) Patriotism is <u>dedication</u> to your <u>country</u>.
> 2) When people feel patriotic, they may be willing to do whatever they feel their country <u>requires</u> of them — including going to <u>war</u>.

Patriotism is sometimes Admired

The Charge of the Light Brigade (Pages 6-7)

1) The men followed the order to charge <u>without question</u>, even though it was clearly a <u>mistake</u> and that "Some one had blunder'd". The poet shows their <u>bravery</u> in doing this with the rhetorical question, "Was there a man dismay'd?".

2) The men are described as <u>loyal</u> and determined to serve their country. The poet respects the "<u>Noble</u> six hundred" and tells us to "<u>Honour</u> the Light Brigade".

But patriotism can also be Dangerous

next to of course god america i (Pages 14-15)

1) The poem focuses on the commanders and politicians who <u>abuse</u> patriotism to create <u>conflict</u> and send people to fight.

2) The speaker tries to get his audience to support him by using lines from <u>patriotic songs</u>.

3) "<u>By jingo</u>" could refer to <u>jingoism</u> — an <u>extreme</u> from of patriotism that encourages <u>armed conflict</u>.

Flag (Pages 18-19)

1) The poem talks about how patriotism, represented by a <u>national flag</u>, can be <u>bad</u>. The flag "brings a nation to its knees", <u>controlling</u> people's behaviour with patriotic ideas.

2) Even though the flag is just "a piece of <u>cloth</u>", it has the power to make men <u>fight</u> and die for their country — it "makes the guts of men grow bold".

'Come On, Come Back' (Pages 8-9)

1) The poem shows that individuals who are <u>fighting</u> against each other because of their patriotism can actually have a lot <u>in common</u>. The enemy sentinel's favourite song was the "Favourite of all the troops of all the armies".

2) Setting the war in the <u>future</u> makes it seem that people will probably <u>go on dying</u> because of patriotism.

Other poems also feature the theme of patriotism...

'At the Border, 1979' shows how strongly <u>attached</u> people can feel to their home country. They are so <u>happy</u> to be back that "A man bent down and kissed his muddy homeland".

Individual Experiences

These poems focus on <u>one person</u>'s experience of conflict, rather than the conflict as a whole.

> 1) Conflicts can involve <u>thousands</u> of people, but everyone involved has their own <u>personal experience</u> of it.
>
> 2) Poets might choose to focus on an individual's experience because it is easier for us as readers to <u>relate</u> to <u>one person</u> rather than a large group.

Some individuals are <u>Directly Affected</u> by conflict

<u>Out of the Blue (Pages 20-21)</u>

1) The poem compares what people might be seeing on <u>television</u> — "a distant shot of a burning building" — with the viewpoint of a <u>victim</u> trapped in one of the towers.
2) What the <u>public</u> is seeing is <u>different</u> to the experience of the <u>victim</u>. The victim is waving for help but sarcastically wonders if the people watching see "a man shaking crumbs / or pegging out washing".

<u>Poppies (Pages 32-33)</u>

1) The poem <u>contrasts</u> the viewpoints of the <u>son</u>, who is "intoxicated", and the <u>mother</u> who is left behind "skirting the church yard walls" and wishing for news.
2) She <u>hides</u> her sadness from her son, saying that she "steeled the softening / of my face" until after he had gone.

People who are <u>Less Involved</u> have a more <u>Detached</u> view

<u>The Right Word (Pages 26-27)</u>

1) The narrator addresses us <u>directly</u> as "you" to <u>make us think</u> about our own attitudes and prejudices.
2) She keeps choosing different words like "<u>terrorist</u>" and "<u>freedom-fighter</u>" to describe the young person, before realising that he's just "<u>a child</u>" — this suggests that we might make <u>poor judgements</u> if we feel under threat.

<u>At the Border, 1979 (Pages 28-29)</u>

1) The poem is written in the <u>first person</u> but is <u>less emotional</u> than the others.
2) The poem explains how a <u>child</u> does not understand the differences between the opposite sides of borders that have been created by <u>adults</u>.
3) Her simple, innocent viewpoint <u>challenges</u> the idea that national boundaries are important.

<u>Other poems also feature individual experiences...</u>

'Come On, Come Back' focuses on <u>Vaudevue</u> and shows how badly she has been affected <u>personally</u> by her experiences of war. 'Bayonet Charge' is about <u>one soldier's</u> personal experience of fighting in a battle that probably involves <u>hundreds</u> or <u>thousands</u> of others.

Death

Death is one of the most popular themes in poetry, especially in poems about conflict.

> 1) Death is an unavoidable part of any armed conflict.
> 2) Death can be described from the point of view of the person who's dying, an outsider, or someone who is causing death.

From the perspective of the Dying Person

Out of the Blue (Pages 20-21)

1) The narrator gets closer and closer to death as the poem goes on, even though he tries to fight against it — he says "I am trying and trying" and "the white of surrender is not yet flying".
2) The narrator seems horrified at the prospect of death as he sees others throw themselves from the building. He says that "The depth is appalling. Appalling".

'Come On, Come Back' (Pages 8-9)

1) Death is presented as something welcome for Vaudevue, because war has been so damaging to her.
2) The lake is described as "adorable", suggesting that it is something positive. When she swims, the current seizes her "in an icy-amorous embrace", as if it's rescuing her from her pain.

From an Outsider's perspective

Mametz Wood (Pages 22-23)

1) The references to death in the poem are surrounded by peaceful images.
2) The descriptions of the way the bones are found help us to imagine the horror of their deaths. The poem describes "their jaws, those that have them" and "their absent tongues" — this reminds us that their bodies have been destroyed by gunfire and by decay.

From the Killer's perspective

Hawk Roosting (Pages 16-17)

1) The hawk has a ruthless approach to the deaths of its victims. The hawk believes it has the right to decide whether other creatures live or die, saying, "I kill where I please because it is all mine".
2) The hawk is proud of its destructive power — it boasts about its "perfect kills".
3) The death the hawk controls sounds violent, but also quick and unemotional — it talks about "tearing off heads".

Other poems also feature the theme of death...

'Futility' is about the death of a young soldier. 'The Charge of the Light Brigade' deals with the deaths of many men. In 'The Falling Leaves' the narrator expresses sadness about the huge numbers of deaths caused by wars. The theme of death also features in 'The Yellow Palm'.

Helplessness

Conflicts can often make the people involved in them feel <u>helpless</u> and <u>powerless</u>.

1) People feel <u>helpless</u> when they're in a situation that they <u>can't control</u>.

2) Sometimes people feel helpless because they are being <u>controlled</u> by other people.

3) Situations like wars also make people feel helpless, because there's <u>nothing</u> they can do to stop them.

Helplessness is caused by <u>Not Being In Control</u>

<u>At the Border, 1979</u> (Pages 28-29)

1) The families in the poem are <u>refugees</u> who are being allowed to return <u>home</u>.

2) They are <u>powerless</u> against the <u>border guards</u> — they have to wait "while our papers were checked, / our faces thoroughly inspected".

<u>Belfast Confetti</u> (Pages 30-31)

1) The narrator is struggling to cope with a situation that is <u>beyond his control</u>. The violent clashes in Belfast often involved <u>innocent citizens</u> like this character.

2) The narrator is feeling physically <u>trapped</u> and finding it hard to <u>think</u> clearly.

3) He is helpless because, although the city is <u>familiar</u> to him ("I know this labyrinth so well"), it has been <u>taken over</u> by security forces and he can't escape.

People are <u>Helpless</u> in the face of <u>Death</u>

<u>Out of the Blue</u> (Pages 20-21)

1) The narrator seems <u>small</u> and <u>unimportant</u> compared to the huge towers of the World Trade Centre. He describes himself as "Small in the clouds" and asks, "Does anyone see / a soul worth saving?"

2) All he can do is <u>wait</u> for help — he asks, "So when will you come?"

3) By the end of the poem he is <u>losing</u> his <u>physical strength</u> — "My arm is numb" — and his <u>emotional strength</u> — "my nerves are sagging".

<u>Futility</u> (Pages 4-5)

1) The <u>title</u> of the poem refers to the <u>uselessness</u> of the attempts to help the soldier. It's clear right from the start of the poem that the narrator <u>won't succeed</u>.

2) Even the sun that "wakes the seeds" is <u>helpless</u> in the face of death and is unable to wake the soldier.

3) The narrator's helplessness makes him <u>angry</u>. His question, "Was it for this the clay grew tall?", suggests that there is <u>no point</u> in creating human life if it's going to end like this.

Other poems also feature the theme of helplessness...

There's a sense of <u>inevitability</u> and helplessness about the deaths in 'The Charge of the Light Brigade' and 'The Falling Leaves'. The mother in 'Poppies' feels helpless because her son is going into a dangerous situation and there's <u>nothing</u> she can do to <u>protect</u> him.

Forms of Poetry

Different <u>forms</u> of poetry are traditionally used to write about different <u>subjects</u>...

> 1) The form and structure a poet chooses affects the <u>message</u> of the poem.
> 2) Poets sometimes deliberately <u>break the rules</u> of how a particular form should be written in order to get their <u>message</u> across.

Ballads tell a Story

The Charge of the Light Brigade (Pages 6-7)

1) Ballads were used to tell <u>stories</u> in a memorable way through strong images. The poet wants the reader to <u>remember</u> the sacrifice made by the Light Brigade.
2) The <u>endings</u> of ballads often have a <u>moral message</u>. Here we are told to "Honour the Light Brigade".
3) Like many ballads, it has a <u>refrain</u> (repeating phrase). It repeats "the six hundred" to remind us of them.

The Yellow Palm (Pages 24-25)

1) This poem uses a more <u>modern</u> ballad form in the <u>first person</u> (using an "I" narrator).
2) Using a <u>refrain</u>, "As I made my way down Palestine Street", reminds the reader that <u>destruction</u> and <u>violence</u> are parts of daily life in an area affected by conflict.

Sonnets are usually about Love

next to of course god america i (Pages 14-15)

1) Traditionally, sonnets were used to write <u>love poetry</u>. Here the subject is <u>patriotic love</u> for a country — "america i / love you".
2) There's a <u>regular rhyme scheme</u>, which is normal for a sonnet, but in this poem it could be <u>ironic</u> considering the <u>jumbled up</u> ideas.
3) Usually the last couplet (pair of lines) <u>sums up</u> the idea of a sonnet. Here, the final line changes to the <u>third person</u> and makes the reader see the speaker <u>differently</u> — we wonder if he's telling the truth.

Sonnets are about love, but the themes of Rupert's poems for Maude were often far 'fruitier'.

Tercets are stanzas with Three Lines

Flag (Pages 18-19)

1) The poet uses each stanza to set up a <u>pattern</u> for the poem.
2) The tercet pattern makes the poem's ideas <u>clear</u>. The <u>contrast</u> between the simple "cloth" and the <u>extreme</u> things people will do for it is highlighted by the <u>short</u> lines and <u>repeated</u> pattern.
3) The pattern changes in the <u>last stanza</u> to make the poet's message <u>clearer</u> — he wants people to see the damage flags can cause.

'Futility' is also written like a sonnet...

'Futility' uses the 14-line sonnet form and the meaning is summed up in the final couplet, which is typical of sonnets. It's about sadness and distress rather than love though.

Poetic Devices

Poets use all kinds of devices to improve their poetry — but not the kind you need a manual for.

> 1) <u>Enjambment</u> means <u>carrying on</u> a sentence or phrase over more than one line. It can be used to draw the reader's <u>attention</u> to important ideas.
>
> 2) <u>Repetition</u> also makes sure that the reader <u>notices</u> key ideas.

Enjambment draws attention to Words and Ideas

Bayonet Charge (Pages 10-11)

1) The <u>enjambment</u> in the poem makes the soldier's <u>panic</u> clear and keeps the pace of the poem <u>fast</u>, as if he can't stop or control himself.
2) The soldier stumbles "towards a green hedge". This doesn't sound threatening until the sentence <u>continues</u> on the next line — it "dazzled with rifle fire". This creates <u>shock</u>.

Belfast Confetti (Pages 30-31)

1) The poet mixes <u>enjambment</u> and <u>end stopping</u> (where phrases end at the end of the line) to suggest someone coming up against <u>dead ends</u>.
2) When the speaker asks, "What is / My name?" the enjambment creates a <u>pause</u> to show how <u>confused</u> he is.

Hawk Roosting (Pages 16-17)

1) Enjambment creates <u>suspense</u> — we wonder what will come next, and what follows is <u>shocking</u> detail in lines like "the one path of my flight is direct / Through the bones of the living."
2) The long sentences and enjambment make the hawk sound as though he is showing off and enjoying being in <u>control</u> — "Now I hold Creation in my foot / Or fly up, and revolve it all slowly".

Repetition highlights Key Ideas

The Right Word (Pages 26-27)

1) The speaker repeats the idea of someone "<u>Outside the door</u>" to show the way that words can create <u>barriers</u> between people.
2) At the end of the poem she repeats the words "<u>Come in</u>". The <u>contrast</u> with "outside" shows that things can <u>change</u> if we change the way we behave.

'Come On, Come Back' (Pages 8-9)

1) The <u>title</u> of the poem is <u>repeated</u> several times and turns out to be a song which is "Favourite of all the troops of all the armies". This shows the <u>similarities</u> between enemies.
2) The poem <u>ends</u> with the title repeated as its last line. It reminds the reader that Vaudevue, and many others, <u>never</u> did come back.

Other poems use interesting sentence structure...

Repetition of words and phrases like "half a league", "cannon" and "the six hundred" in 'The Charge of the Light Brigade' suggests that the events that are described in the poem were inevitable.

Poetic Devices

Even more poetic devices — hurray...

> 1) Sound effects like <u>alliteration</u> (repeating consonant sounds) produce a particular <u>effect</u> in a poem.
>
> 2) Other language features like unusual or unexpected <u>vocabulary</u> can also add extra <u>impact</u> to a poem.

Poetic Devices *can Add to the Emotion of a poem*

Mametz Wood (Pages 22-23)

1) <u>Assonance</u> (repeating vowel sounds) and <u>alliteration</u> are used in the poem. "A <u>ch</u>it of bone, the <u>ch</u>ina plate of a shoulder blade", sounds like the <u>pl</u>ough hitting the soldiers' skeletons in the soil.

2) Words with <u>double meanings</u> add to the thoughtful tone of the poem. "<u>Relic</u>" is a religious word, so makes the soldiers sound like <u>saints</u>, and the "<u>foreign body</u>" is the body of a <u>foreign soldier</u>.

The Falling Leaves (Pages 12-13)

1) The poet uses <u>alliteration</u> to describe the leaves falling "<u>W</u>hen no <u>w</u>ind <u>w</u>hirled them <u>w</u>histling to the sky". This creates a sense of <u>movement</u> which contrasts with "a still afternoon".

2) <u>Assonance</u> is used to show an <u>important idea</u> in the poem. The soldiers "now all withering l<u>ay</u>, / Sl<u>ai</u>n" — the repeating vowel sound in "lay" and "slain" makes the reader focus on these words, making the description more <u>shocking</u>.

Unusual Vocabulary *can make the poet's Point Clearer*

next to of course god america i (Pages 14-15)

1) The poem mixes <u>persuasive</u> language with casual <u>slang</u>. The speaker seems to be trying to please <u>everyone</u> by using a range of language styles, but it makes him seem <u>false</u>.

2) Some phrases are <u>not quite correct</u> — e.g. "deafanddumb" and "by gorry" — as if the speaker is not really thinking about what he's saying.

3) Some phrases sound very <u>old-fashioned</u> and <u>formal</u> — e.g. "thy sons acclaim your glorious name". The speaker is using formal language to sound <u>important</u> and <u>clever</u>.

'Come On, Come Back' (Pages 8-9)

1) Using <u>strange</u> names like "Vaudevue" and "M.L.5." reinforces the <u>strangeness</u> of the setting.

2) Long sentences and alliteration change the <u>pace</u> of the poem. It speeds up when Vaudevue goes into the lake — "She strips her uniform off, strips, stands and plunges", creating sudden <u>drama</u>.

'Out of the Blue' also uses these language features...

Alliteration in 'Out of the Blue' makes the reader focus on important movements such as "twirling, turning" and "wind-milling, wheeling". Repetition makes the narrator's emotions more intense.

Rhyme and Rhythm

Rhyming is fun — rhyme, time, slime, crime... Nothing really rhymes with "rhythm" though.

1) Rhyme and rhythm have an effect on how a poem <u>sounds</u>, which can add to the <u>meaning</u>.
2) They can also be used to <u>highlight</u> key words and ideas.

Some poems have a Regular Rhyme and Rhythm

The Charge of the Light Brigade (Pages 6-7)

1) The poet uses <u>regular rhythm</u> all the way through the poem to suggest a sense of the <u>energy</u> and <u>speed</u> of the cavalry charging forward into battle.
2) The rhythm sounds like the <u>galloping</u> of horses' hooves.
3) All the stanzas contain <u>rhymes</u> and <u>consonance</u> such as "onward", "blunder'd" and "thunder'd", which highlight the <u>final rhyme</u> in each stanza and the <u>number</u> of men involved.

The Yellow Palm (Pages 24-25)

A slow pace can be annoying if you're in a hurry.

1) The second, fourth and sixth lines in each stanza rhyme. This helps to <u>emphasise</u> the <u>final line</u> in each stanza — usually the ones that mention a negative detail.
2) The poet uses rhyme to highlight <u>key words</u> and ideas. He rhymes "prayer" with "despair", and "smile" with "missile", to show how the city has been <u>changed</u> by war.
3) The rhythm of each stanza is fairly regular and creates a <u>slow pace</u>. This makes it seem like the narrator is <u>stopping</u> every so often as he wanders along the street.

Irregular rhyme and rhythm Add to the Meaning of poems

'Come On, Come Back' (Pages 8-9)

1) The rhyme and rhythm in the poem are <u>irregular</u> — this reflects Vaudevue's <u>confusion</u>.
2) <u>Internal rhymes</u> (rhyming words in the same line) create a <u>creepy</u> tone and emphasise the imagery in lines like "At midnight in the moonlight".

Out of the Blue (Pages 20-21)

1) The poet uses a lot of <u>rhyme</u> and <u>internal rhyme</u>.
2) He uses rhyme to <u>highlight</u> some of the harsher words such as "driving" and "diving".
3) <u>Half-rhymes</u> within a sentence — e.g. "leaving, diving" — make the poem sound <u>urgent</u>.
4) The slow rhythm of the <u>long vowel sounds</u> of "wind-milling, wheeling, spiralling, falling" show the reader how far the victims are falling.

'Futility' uses half-rhyme instead of full rhyme...

'Futility' mostly uses half-rhyme (e.g. "seeds" and "sides"), but the final line of each stanza rhymes with the fifth line — this produces a sense of completeness at the end of each stanza.

Use of First Person

Lots of poets use a first-person narrator to get their <u>message</u> across more strongly.

> 1) The <u>viewpoint</u> the poem is narrated from affects the way it comes across to the <u>reader</u>.
> 2) A <u>first-person ("I") narrator</u> often makes a poem seem more <u>personal</u> and <u>emotional</u>.
> 3) Description using the <u>first-person</u> may be more <u>one-sided</u> than third-person descriptions.

First-Person Narration *can seem more Personal*

Poppies (Pages 32-33)

1) The character speaking in this poem is a <u>mother</u> whose son has left home to fight in the army.
2) The use of the first person allows the poet to express the mother's <u>strong emotions</u>, e.g. "I was brave, as I walked / with you, to the front door". The poem seems very <u>personal</u>, as if she is revealing her most private thoughts.

Out of the Blue (Pages 20-21)

1) Using the first person makes the character's horror seem more <u>real</u> and <u>upsetting</u>.
2) It reminds the reader that the victims of the World Trade Centre attacks were all <u>real people</u> with lives and <u>families</u>, not just tiny figures on a television screen.
3) The first-person voice lets the reader see the <u>changing emotions</u> of someone trapped in the disaster. The narrator starts off sounding <u>determined to survive</u> — "the white of surrender is not yet flying" — but then begins to <u>lose hope</u> and is "tiring, tiring".

The Right Word (Pages 26-27)

1) The poem is in the first person but the speaker could represent <u>anyone</u>, including the reader. The poet emphasises this by repeating <u>personal pronouns</u> — "I", "my", "mine", "your" and "you".
2) The speaker <u>asks</u> the reader directly, "Is that the wrong description?", which makes the reader think about the idea that words can be <u>confusing</u> and give the wrong impression.

But First-Person Narrators *can be Unreliable*

Hawk Roosting (Pages 16-17)

1) The poem is written in the voice of a <u>hawk</u>. The language it uses is <u>blunt</u> and <u>self-centred</u> to create a sense of the hawk's <u>power</u> and <u>arrogance</u>.
2) Although the hawk is giving its view of the world, the way the poem is written makes it obvious that it is <u>not as powerful</u> as it thinks.

Changing a poem's perspective can change its meaning...

If 'At the Border, 1979' had been narrated from the mother's point of view rather than the child's, the effect of the poem would have been to praise her homeland rather than to criticise borders.

Beginnings of Poems

Poets have to make sure that the beginning of the poem makes us want to keep reading.

> 1) The beginning of the poem is important because it <u>sets the tone</u> for the rest of the poem.
>
> 2) Poets try to get the reader's <u>attention</u> straight away, using techniques like <u>talking to</u> the reader directly or sounding <u>mysterious</u>.

Beginnings can be Dramatic

Futility (Pages 4-5)

1) This poem <u>involves</u> the reader immediately by beginning with an <u>order</u>.
2) The <u>beginning</u> of the poem creates questions in the reader's mind — the pronoun "him" is <u>mysterious</u>, and we have to <u>guess</u> who the character is and why he can't move himself.

Bayonet Charge (Pages 10-11)

1) The poem begins with the word "<u>Suddenly</u>", which creates the sense of <u>urgency</u> and panic that the soldier is feeling.
2) It starts in the middle of the <u>action</u>, putting the reader in the same <u>confused</u> position as the soldier who "awoke" to find himself in a battle.

Mopsy only liked poems with dramatic beginnings.

Beginnings can introduce a Theme

Mametz Wood (Pages 22-23)

1) The poem begins with the idea that an event has <u>already happened</u>.
   The word "afterwards" refers to the <u>war</u>, but that might not be obvious to start with.
2) The poet uses a <u>pronoun</u> — "them" — to make the reader wonder who this refers to.
   The answer — "the wasted young" — is <u>shocking</u> compared to the relaxed feel of the opening.
3) The first stanza introduces the idea of <u>damage</u> and loss.
   The word "wasted" suggests decay and <u>pointless loss</u> of young lives.
4) The farmers "tended the land back into itself". This introduces the idea that the land has been injured and <u>damaged</u> by the fighting, which is described in more detail later in the poem.

'The Charge of the Light Brigade' has a good beginning too...

The opening lines of 'The Charge of the Light Brigade' — "Half a league, half a league, / Half a league onward" — give the impression of rushing non-stop towards their doom.

Couplets and Last Lines

Last lines are pretty <u>important</u> too...

> 1) The last line of a poem's important, because the reader's most likely to <u>remember</u> the ending.
>
> 2) Poets might try to <u>sum up</u> the poem at the end so that the reader remembers the <u>message</u>.

Closing couplets can Sum Up a Message

The Charge of the Light Brigade (Pages 6-7)

1) The last line sums up how the Light Brigade should be <u>remembered</u> — as the "<u>Noble</u> six hundred!"
2) The exclamation mark makes the adjective "Noble" <u>stand out</u>.
3) The poet uses a <u>rhyming couplet</u> just before the last line. The rhyme and repetition emphasise the command to "<u>Honour</u> the Light Brigade".

Flag (Pages 18-19)

1) The final couplet of the poem sounds very <u>sarcastic</u> and <u>cynical</u>.
2) The couplet is used to <u>sum up</u> and emphasise the message of the poem. The speaker is warning the listener that <u>loyalty</u> to a country's flag can make people do <u>immoral</u> things like killing people — "blind your conscience to the end".
3) Making the last two lines a rhyming couplet is a <u>change</u> from the rhyme scheme of the previous stanzas. It makes the ending sound more <u>definite</u>.

Endings can Create a Contrast

At the Border, 1979 (Pages 28-29)

1) The last line in this poem uses an image of a "<u>chain of mountains</u>" to sum up the poet's <u>message</u> about man-made borders. The word "chain" reminds the reader of the "thick iron chain" earlier on in the poem which was <u>trapping</u> the family.
2) However, this chain of mountains "encompassed all of us" — it <u>joins</u> people rather than dividing them.
3) The <u>straightforward</u>, <u>simple</u> feel of the final statement makes the poet's message seem <u>obvious</u> — man-made divisions are pointless.

The Yellow Palm (Pages 24-25)

1) The poem ends with a simple and <u>innocent</u> image. The picture of the child reaching out and receiving fruit is a <u>contrast</u> to the way war has made other parts of life so complicated.
2) The language is <u>plain</u>. The poet could be suggesting that a simple change in <u>behaviour</u> could <u>solve</u> many of the problems of war.

Other poems have significant last lines...

The final two lines in 'Out of the Blue' emphasise "sagging" and "flagging", making the narrator sound like he's given up. 'Futility' ends with a question that challenges the reader.

Imagery

They say a picture paints a thousand words. Well, sometimes words can paint a picture too...

> 1) Imagery is language that describes a particular <u>sense</u>
>   — sight, smell, sound, taste or touch.
> 2) <u>Metaphors</u> and <u>similes compare</u> the thing being described to something else.

Imagery can be Violent

Bayonet Charge (Pages 10-11)

1) The imagery in this poem is <u>violent</u> and <u>painful</u>. Similes like "lugged a rifle numb as a smashed arm" suggest <u>pain</u> and make the soldier's body and his weapon seem to <u>blur</u> together.
2) By describing things that the soldier <u>sees</u>, <u>hears</u> and <u>feels</u>, the poet makes the soldier's situation seem more <u>realistic</u> and <u>scary</u> — e.g. "dazzled with rifle fire", "Bullets smacking the belly out of the air", "blue crackling air".
3) The poet uses a metaphor to describe the "cold clockwork of the stars and the nations". This makes the soldier seem very <u>small</u> and <u>unimportant</u> in such a huge world.

Belfast Confetti (Pages 30-31)

Nicki mixed weapon imagery with eccentric clothes and make-up.

1) The narrator in this poem uses the imagery of <u>writing</u> to explain the experience of being caught up in <u>violence</u> in Belfast. He makes language seem <u>aggressive</u> and dangerous.
2) "A fount of broken type" and "it was raining exclamation marks" describe the painful <u>shrapnel</u> and <u>debris</u> from the explosion which shower down on him.
3) He mixes <u>language</u> and <u>weapon</u> imagery to describe his experiences. The metaphor "A fusillade of question-marks" makes it sound like he is being <u>attacked by language</u>.

Images can create a Reflective mood

Mametz Wood (Pages 22-23)

1) The imagery makes the soldiers' bones sound <u>fragile</u> and <u>delicate</u> — e.g. "the blown / and broken bird's egg of a skull" and "the china plate of a shoulder blade".
2) The poet uses the image of a <u>wound</u> "working a foreign body to the surface of the skin" to describe the soldiers' remains being unearthed — as if the land wants them to be <u>discovered</u>.
3) The poet combines images of <u>horror</u> and <u>beauty</u>. He talks about "the notes they had sung", which sounds gentle, but their "absent tongues" remind the reader that they have rotted away.
4) The <u>image</u> of "nesting machine guns" creates a contrast with the peaceful natural images and shows how war has damaged the natural landscape.

'Poppies' and 'The Falling Leaves' also use imagery...

Military imagery in 'Poppies' reminds us that the son is going to war. The mother uses housework imagery to describe her fear. In 'The Falling Leaves', leaves and snowflakes represent dead soldiers.

<u>Irony</u>

Like rain on your wedding day... (That's actually not ironic at all, just bad luck.)

> 1) Poems are ironic if what a narrator or character says is <u>different</u> from what they <u>mean</u>.
>
> 2) Poets often use irony to make <u>views</u> that they strongly <u>disagree</u> with seem <u>ridiculous</u>.

These poems treat <u>Patriotism</u> in an <u>Ironic way</u>

<u>Flag (Pages 18-19)</u>

1) The poem suggests it's ironic that even though a flag is "just a piece of <u>cloth</u>" it can have such <u>power</u> that it can bring "a nation to its knees".
2) The speaker uses an <u>ironic tone</u> when he says that to get hold of something so powerful, all his questioner has to do is "Just ask for a flag, my friend".
3) The message of the poem is that <u>patriotism</u> (love for your country) can be <u>dangerous</u>.

<u>next to of course god america i (Pages 14-15)</u>

1) The poem is written in an ironic way. The speaker in the poem is trying to seem <u>inspirational</u> and honest, but the poet wants the reader to see him as <u>false</u>.
2) At the end of his speech the speaker asks, "then shall the voice of liberty be mute?"
3) This is meant to be a powerful <u>rhetorical question</u> (a question that the speaker thinks has an obvious answer) that makes his audience support him — but it's ironic because the line before is all about how those who have fought before are <u>dead</u> — their voices really are <u>mute</u>.

<u>At the Border, 1979 (Pages 28-29)</u>

1) The irony is that the <u>adults</u> in the poem are very <u>emotional</u> about crossing the border back to their homeland, while the narrator can see that the land in both countries is <u>the same</u>.
2) The narrator reports what her parents have told her in a <u>straightforward</u> way that makes them seem a bit <u>silly</u>. E.g. it seems unlikely that "soon everything would taste different".
3) The last line sums up the irony — "The <u>same</u> chain of mountains encompassed all of us."

Irony can <u>Highlight Violence</u> and <u>Horror</u>

<u>Belfast Confetti (Pages 30-31)</u>

1) The <u>title</u> of this poem is ironic. Confetti is associated with <u>celebration</u> and happiness, especially at weddings, which usually <u>bring people together</u>. But Belfast confetti refers to <u>shrapnel</u> of bombs and the idea that groups of people are <u>divided</u>.
2) It's ironic that the character in the poem can list the names of <u>military equipment</u>, e.g."Saracen" and "Kremlin-2 mesh", but he can't remember his own <u>name</u> or where he is going.

'Come On, Come Back' is ironic too...

'Come On, Come Back' suggests that it's ironic that people join enemy armies when they have things in common — Vaudevue and the enemy sentinel have the same favourite song.

Mood

After all this revision I'd guess you're in a pretty bad mood...

> 1) Mood in poetry is about the <u>tone</u> or <u>atmosphere</u> of the poem.
> 2) Most of the poems to do with conflict have a <u>sad</u> or <u>angry</u> tone because they deal with a <u>negative topic</u>.

Most of these poems have a Sad Mood

Futility (Pages 4-5)

1) The mood of this poem is one of <u>sadness</u> at the waste of human life in war.
2) The narrator's tone becomes more <u>bitter</u> and <u>disillusioned</u> as the poem goes on. He begins by talking about the "kind old sun", but by the end he is <u>criticising</u> the "fatuous sunbeams".
3) The poem develops a <u>challenging</u> tone as the speaker asks what is the point of life when it can be so easily destroyed by war. The final question sounds <u>angry</u>.

Come On, Come Back (Pages 8-9)

1) The mood of the poem is <u>sad</u> for Vaudevue's lost life.
2) There is a <u>lonely</u> atmosphere in the poem. Vaudevue's mind is "secret from her". The enemy sentinel waits <u>alone</u> for her return, which never happens. Her clothes are "<u>abandoned</u>".
3) The waters that Vaudevue drowns in are <u>welcoming</u> to her, but the description of them also creates a <u>dark</u>, <u>grim</u> mood — they are "black as her mind".

Meg preferred a mood of loud sadness.

The Falling Leaves (Pages 12-13)

1) This poem has a mood of <u>quiet sadness</u>.
2) The focus is on <u>death</u> right from the beginning. The poet describes the dead "brown leaves dropping" like the dead soldiers who "all withering lay".
3) The images of the leaves falling <u>in silence</u> and the snowflakes "wiping out the noon" create a <u>peaceful</u> atmosphere in the middle of the poem.
4) There is a tone of <u>respect</u> and <u>admiration</u> for the men. The poet calls them a "gallant multitude".

Some have a Worried Mood

Poppies (Pages 32-33)

1) The poem starts in a <u>serious</u> mood. It is "Three days before Armistice Sunday", which immediately reminds the reader of all the people who have <u>died</u> in wars.
2) The mother in the poem wants to express her real feelings, but she <u>hides</u> her emotions from her son.
3) There is an atmosphere of <u>fear</u> and <u>anxiety</u> that the mother is <u>holding back</u> in the poem.
4) The mother's anxious mood <u>contrasts</u> with the son's <u>excitement</u> — he is "intoxicated".

All poems have a mood...

The mood of 'Flag' is calm and sarcastic; the mood of 'The Charge of the Light Brigade' is respect and admiration; the mood of 'Bayonet Charge' and 'Belfast Confetti' is fear and panic.

Section Four — Poetry Techniques

The Poetry Exam: Unit Two Overview

If you're following <u>Route A</u> of the AQA English Literature course, you'll have to do an <u>exam</u> called <u>Unit 2: Poetry Across Time</u>. That's what this page is all about.

Your Exam Will be Split Up Like This

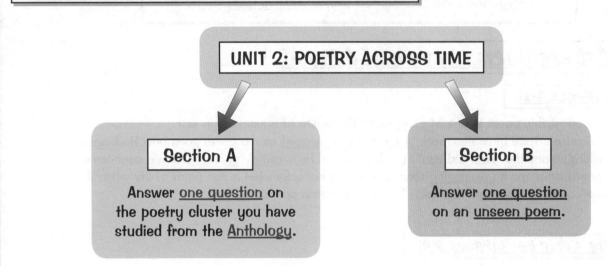

UNIT 2: POETRY ACROSS TIME

Section A

Answer <u>one question</u> on the poetry cluster you have studied from the <u>Anthology</u>.

Section B

Answer <u>one question</u> on an <u>unseen poem</u>.

1) This guide contains all the poems from the '<u>Conflict</u>' cluster of the Anthology — this should be the one you've studied in class. There are three other poetry clusters, which you <u>don't</u> need to <u>worry about</u>.

2) The next few pages will give you <u>tips</u> on how to answer the question in <u>Section A</u>.

3) Section A is worth <u>two-thirds</u> of the marks in the <u>exam</u> and nearly a <u>quarter</u> of your entire <u>GCSE</u>.

This is How Your Exam Will Work

1) The whole exam lasts <u>1 hour 15 minutes</u>. You should spend about <u>45 minutes</u> on <u>Section A</u>. The other 30 minutes should be spent doing Section B.

2) Section A has a <u>choice</u> of <u>two questions</u> for each poetry cluster. You should only answer <u>one</u> <u>question</u> and it should be about the cluster you've <u>studied</u>. The question is worth <u>36 marks</u>.

3) You're <u>not allowed</u> to take your <u>own anthology</u> or any <u>notes</u> about the poems into the exam. You'll be given a <u>blank copy</u> of the anthology to help you with your answer.

4) You'll also be given a <u>separate answer book</u> to write your answer in.

There are Instructions on the Front Page of the Exam

1) You <u>must read</u> the <u>front page</u> of the exam paper <u>before</u> you start — it tells you <u>exactly</u> what to do.

2) There will be a <u>list</u> of things you need for the exam. Make sure you've got <u>everything</u> on it.

3) Check you've got the <u>right exam paper</u> — it should be the one for the <u>foundation tier</u>.

4) Remember to fill in <u>all the details</u> on the front page of the <u>answer booklet</u>.

I hope you're paying attention — there's an exam on this...

I like pages like this. Absolutely <u>no learning</u> whatsoever. Lovely. Don't worry if you forget some of this stuff — there'll be a <u>reminder</u> of how the exam works on the <u>front page</u> of the exam paper.

Sample Question 1

OK, so now you know what the <u>exam's about</u>. I bet you're just <u>dying</u> to find out what the questions will be like, eh? Er, well... Here's your <u>first sample question</u> anyway.

Read the Question Carefully and Underline Key Words

1) You'll have a <u>choice</u> of <u>two questions</u>, so it's best to <u>read</u> them both through <u>carefully</u> first. Then pick the one you think you've got the <u>best chance</u> of answering well.

2) Once you've done that, <u>read</u> the question you've chosen through <u>again</u>. <u>Underline</u> the question's <u>theme</u> and any other important words.

3) The question will give you the title of <u>one poem</u> and ask you to <u>compare</u> it to <u>one other</u> poem of <u>your choice</u>. Pick another poem you think relates to the theme.

4) <u>Look up</u> the poems you're going to write about in the <u>blank copy</u> of the <u>anthology</u> you'll be given in the exam. <u>Turn over the corners</u> of the pages they're on so you can find them again <u>quickly</u>.

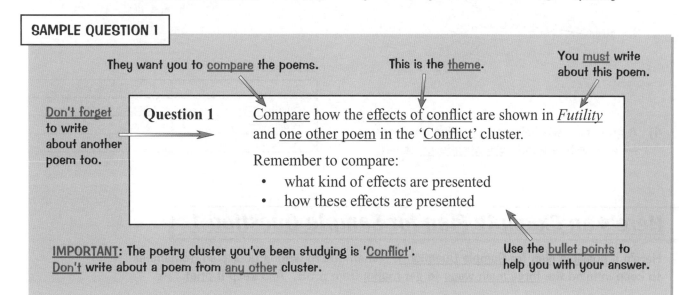

SAMPLE QUESTION 1

They want you to <u>compare</u> the poems.

This is the <u>theme</u>.

You <u>must</u> write about this poem.

<u>Don't forget</u> to write about another poem too.

Question 1   Compare how the <u>effects of conflict</u> are shown in *Futility* and <u>one other poem</u> in the 'Conflict' cluster.

Remember to compare:
* what kind of effects are presented
* how these effects are presented

<u>IMPORTANT</u>: The poetry cluster you've been studying is '<u>Conflict</u>'. <u>Don't</u> write about a poem from <u>any other</u> cluster.

Use the <u>bullet points</u> to help you with your answer.

There are Three Main Ways to Get Marks

<u>Whichever</u> question you choose to answer, you'll get marks for:

① Giving your own <u>thoughts</u> and <u>opinions</u> on the poems and supporting them with <u>quotes</u> from the text.

② <u>Explaining</u> the effects of features like <u>form</u>, <u>structure</u> and <u>language</u>.

③ Describing the <u>similarities</u> and <u>differences</u> between poems.

Keep these <u>three things</u> in mind when you're <u>writing</u> and <u>planning</u> your answer.

You'll also pick up marks for writing clearly with good spelling and punctuation.

In 18th century Scotland, the penalty for forgetting to include quotes was severe.

Read the question carefully...

If only I'd always followed that particular <u>piece of advice</u> myself — there might never have been that <u>unfortunate incident</u> with the policeman and the chocolate orange. Still, we live and learn.

Planning

If you were to ask me what my best tip would be for getting great marks in your exam, I would not say, "bribe the examiner". Oh no. That would be wrong. I'd say, "plan your essay answer".

Spend Five Minutes Planning Your Answer

1) Always plan your answer before you start — that way, you're less likely to forget something important.

2) Write your plan at the top of your answer booklet and draw a neat line through it when you've finished.

3) Don't spend too long on your plan. It's only rough work, so you don't need to write in full sentences. Here are a few examples of different ways you can plan your answer:

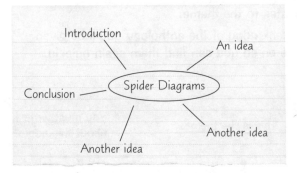

Bullet points with...
- Intro...
- An idea...
- The next idea...

Tables with...

A point...	Quote to back this up...
Another point...	Quote...
A different point...	Quote...
A brand new point...	Quote...

4) A good plan will help you organise your ideas — and write a good, well-structured essay.

Here's an Example Plan for Sample Question 1

Here's a possible plan for Sample Question 1. When you're writing your plan, remember to keep in mind the three main ways to get marks from p.55. And keep it brief.

Plan: poem 1 = Futility, poem 2 = Mametz Wood

1) Introduction — the kind of effects in each poem
- Poem 1 — soldier killed in World War 1
- Poem 2 — dug up forgotten remains, also from World War 1

2) Language Comparison — how the effects are presented
- Poem 1 — imagery shows care and compassion — "kind"
- Poem 2 — imagery shows emptiness, fragility — "wasted", "broken bird's egg"

3) Form and Structure Comparison — how the effects are presented
- Poem 1 — half-rhymes, seems natural
- Poem 2 — no regular rhyme scheme, short 3-line stanzas

4) Message — why poem was written
- Poem 1 — shows futility of war through death of soldier
- Poem 2 — remembers past using lost war graves

5) Summary — Comparing — 'Both these poems...'

Use your plan to start making links between the poems.

Jot down any good quotes you want to use.

Don't forget to write about language, structure and form.

Write about ideas and attitudes too.

You can't write a great essay without a good plan...

This is time well spent — five minutes spent planning your answer in an exam will help you get a much better mark. Practise by planning your own answers to the sample questions in this guide.

THIS IS A FLAP.
FOLD THIS PAGE OUT.

How to Answer the Question

3 Form and Structure
full rhymes. The first stanza describes helping the soldier, but in the second stanza the narrator realises his friend is beyond help. This lets the poet end with his angry rhetorical question about the effects of war. 'Mametz Wood', on the other hand, is written in tercets with no regular rhyme scheme. It switches between describing what is happening in the present — the skeletons being discovered — and what happened in the past. This emphasises how the effects of war are long-lasting.

Don't just describe the technique — explain its effect too.

4 Message
Although 'Futility' and 'Mametz Wood' were written many years apart, they both explore the terrible effects of conflict. Wilfred Owen uses his poem to present the idea that war is a tragic waste of life. Part of the reason it does this so well is because Owen witnessed war in the trenches first-hand. As a soldier, he probably saw many deaths like the one he describes in 'Futility'. It is easy to see how this would have affected him and why he would have wanted people to know how sad and pointless war really is. Owen Sheers never saw the conflict, but he also manages to effectively present the horrors of war to the reader. His poem is about encouraging the reader to remember the "wasted young" who lost their lives in battle. Both poets may have felt that by telling people about the terrible effects of war, it would help stop conflict like this from happening again.

Give your own interpretation of the poem's message.

Keep making comparisons.

5 Conclusion
'Futility' and 'Mametz Wood' clearly show that suffering and tragedy are both effects of conflict. They both make use of vivid imagery to remind us that war often results in a pointless waste of young lives that are not to be forgotten.

It's a good idea to end by referring to both poems.

How to Answer the Question

Here's a 'C' grade sample answer to the exam question on p.55.

<u>Compare how the effects of conflict are shown in 'Futility'
and one other poem in the 'Conflict' cluster.</u>

<u>Remember to compare:</u>
- <u>what kind of effects are presented</u>
- <u>how these effects are presented</u>

Don't forget to follow the advice in the bullet points.

1 Introduction

Conflict can have many terrible effects. In 'Futility', Wilfred Owen describes a soldier who has been killed in a World War I battle. In 'Mametz Wood', Owen Sheers describes rediscovering lost World War I war graves in order to remind us of what happened. Both Owen and Sheers explore the sad waste of life that is always an effect of war.

Tell the examiner how both poems relate to the theme.

2 Language

Both poets use imagery to describe their thoughts and feelings about the effects of war. Wilfred Owen personifies the sun and hopes that it can bring his wounded friend back to life because "its touch awoke him once". He links the sun with life itself when he says: "If anything might rouse him now / The kind old sun will know". The poet questions why the sun created life in the first place, just so that it would be taken away in battle: "O what made fatuous sunbeams toil / To break earth's sleep at all?" He seems to be suggesting that war has made the sunbeams' hard work foolish and pointless. Owen Sheers also uses personification in his poem when he writes that "the earth stands sentinel", guarding the bones of the soldiers who are buried in it. He emphasises how fragile life is with his descriptions of the soldiers' remains, for example: "the china plate of a shoulder blade" and the "broken bird's egg of a skull". The bird imagery is continued when the soldiers are ordered towards "nesting machine guns". Nesting is normally associated with eggs and new life, but here there is just death. These images show us how horrible and brutal the effects of conflict can be.

Talk about similarities and differences between the two poems.

Back up your points with quotes from the poem.

Describe the effect of different images.

The form and structure of both poems also affects the way the results of war are presented. 'Futility' is a bit like a sonnet, but it has two halves and the rhymes are mainly half-rhymes rather than

Use technical terms where you can.

Mark Scheme

If I were you, I'd be pretty keen to find out what the examiner expected of me right about now. Oh yes, it'd definitely feature somewhere in my top 20 things to do when bored. Maybe top 50.

Look at What You Have to Do to Get Each Grade

Here are the kinds of things you'll need to do to get different grades.
You'll need to match most or all of these to get the grade they describe.

Grade	What you've written
C	• Comments clearly on several aspects of the poems, e.g. mood, language, feelings, and uses quotes to back the comments up • Makes plenty of comparisons between the poems • Explains how language, form and structure affect the reader • Makes valid comments about themes, attitudes or feelings in the poems
D	• Comments clearly on the poems and uses quotes to back up several points • Makes several comparisons between the poems • Identifies the effects of language, form and structure on the reader • Talks about some of the themes, attitudes or feelings in the poems
E	• Comments on the poems and uses occasional quotes to back up some points • Makes occasional comparisons between the poems • Shows some understanding of language, form or structure • Gives a rough overview of the themes, attitudes or feelings in the poems
F	• Makes some comments about the poems, mentioning some details from the text • Occasionally makes simple links between the poems • Shows a basic understanding of language, form or structure • Mentions some of the themes, attitudes or feelings in the poems
G	• Makes a simple comment (or comments) about the poems • May suggest a link between the poems • Mentions something about language, form or structure • May mention one of the themes, attitudes or feelings in the poems

> You'll also be marked on your spelling, punctuation and grammar.
> To get the most marks your work should be clear and easy to understand.

Section Five — The Poetry Exam

Sample Question 2

Okey-doke, here's another <u>Sample Question</u> for you — it's <u>number two</u> of <u>three</u>, you lucky thing. Have a think about how <u>you'd</u> answer it, then turn over for an <u>example</u> of how you could do it.

Here's Sample Question 2

This is another <u>example</u> of the type of question that might come up in your <u>exam</u>.
Remember to <u>read</u> the question <u>carefully</u> and <u>underline key words</u>.

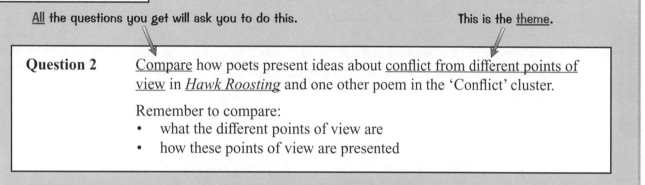

SAMPLE QUESTION 2

<u>All</u> the questions you get will ask you to do this.

This is the <u>theme</u>.

Question 2   <u>Compare</u> how poets present ideas about <u>conflict from different points of view</u> in *Hawk Roosting* and one other poem in the 'Conflict' cluster.

Remember to compare:
* what the different points of view are
* how these points of view are presented

<u>REMEMBER</u>: you <u>must</u> write about <u>Hawk Roosting</u> and one other poem.

Here's an Example Plan for Sample Question 2

Here's an example of a <u>different way</u> you could plan your answer. Remember, you need to start thinking up <u>comparisons</u> between the poems at the <u>planning stage</u>.

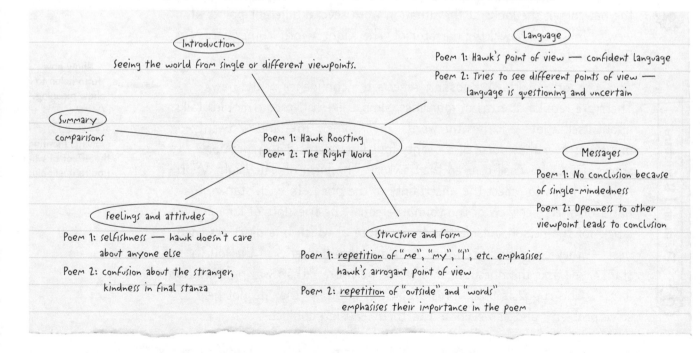

Introduction
Seeing the world from single or different viewpoints.

Language
Poem 1: Hawk's point of view — confident language
Poem 2: Tries to see different points of view — language is questioning and uncertain

Summary
comparisons

Poem 1: Hawk Roosting
Poem 2: The Right Word

Messages
Poem 1: No conclusion because of single-mindedness
Poem 2: Openness to other viewpoint leads to conclusion

feelings and attitudes
Poem 1: selfishness — hawk doesn't care about anyone else
Poem 2: confusion about the stranger, kindness in final stanza

Structure and form
Poem 1: *repetition* of "me", "my", "I", etc. emphasises hawk's arrogant point of view
Poem 2: *repetition* of "outside" and "words" emphasises their importance in the poem

Try out different types of plans to see what's best for you...

When you're writing answers to <u>practice exam questions</u>, try doing your <u>plan</u> a bit <u>differently</u> each time — that way, you can work out the <u>best way</u> to <u>organise your ideas</u> before the real thing.

Section Five — The Poetry Exam

How to Answer the Question

Here's a 'C' grade sample answer to the exam question on p.59.

Compare how poets present ideas about conflict from different points of view in 'Hawk Roosting' and one other poem in the 'Conflict' cluster.

Remember to compare:
* what the different points of view are
* how these points of view are presented

1 Introduction

Some people see the world from a particular point of view and refuse to look at it from a different angle — this can sometimes cause conflict. Others are more open-minded and avoid conflict by making an effort to see things from a different person's perspective. This is the subject of the poems 'Hawk Roosting' and 'The Right Word'.

Show that you understand the question.

2 Language

Ted Hughes's 'Hawk Roosting' presents the single-mindedness of a hawk from the hawk's point of view. The bird believes that the whole of "Creation" exists just for itself, and describes using its power to cause conflict and violence — it is happy about making "perfect kills" and "tearing off heads". The hawk believes that it controls everything around it and has never considered a different point of view. In contrast, 'The Right Word' by Imtiaz Dharker is full of uncertainty. The narrator asks lots of questions as she attempts to work out who or what is standing outside the door. As the speaker searches for the "right way" to describe the newcomer, she looks at the situation from several different points of view. Unlike the hawk, the narrator of 'The Right Word' comes across as fearful and vulnerable.

Use quotes to support your ideas.

3 Form and Structure

The form of 'Hawk Roosting' reflects the confidence of the hawk. There are regular stanzas of four lines, almost like a hymn. The bird talks about itself a lot — it uses the words "me", "mine", "my" and "I" twenty-one times over the course of a twenty-four line poem. This repetition shows us just how self-centred the hawk is. The form of 'The Right Word', however, helps to reflect the uncertainty of the poet. In each stanza, the narrator alters her view of the young person. She tries lots of different labels for the person outside the door, unsure of which one describes them best — they could be a "terrorist" or a "freedom-fighter". In the fourth stanza, she asks the question: "Are words no more / than waving, wavering flags?" This suggests that words are just symbols — they do not help to solve problems and can even add to them, causing conflict.

Show how form helps to show meaning.

Always mention the effect of what you're describing.

How to Answer the Question

Feelings and Attitudes

4

The emotions in the two poems also show contrasting points of view about conflict. The confusion and frustration of the narrator in 'The Right Word' is shown in questions like "Is that the wrong description?", and in outbursts such as "God help me". The uncertain attitude of the narrator in 'The Right Word' is very different to Ted Hughes's hawk. The hawk has a very clear sense of its purpose and its place in the world. It believes the whole world exists just for it and claims ownership of all of nature: "Now I hold Creation in my foot." In spite of this, the reader is left in no doubt about the foolishness of the hawk's point of view when it says, "I am going to keep things like this." We know that in the real world this is impossible.

Remember to keep making comparisons.

Messages

5

In 'The Right Word', the narrator's conclusion is quite different from that of 'Hawk Roosting'. In 'The Right Word', the narrator's point of view about the stranger is finally decided when she invites the child outside the door into her home. She then learns that the child is a good person who "carefully... / takes off his shoes" before he comes in. This is a very trusting way to resolve the narrator's problem. The stranger is no longer threatening after a simple act of friendship. Ted Hughes's hawk, on the other hand, makes no effort to see things from anybody else's point of view. The hawk is confident that it can control everything around it. This poet might be comparing the hawk's behaviour to the way political leaders sometimes behave. He could be suggesting that refusing to see anyone else's point of view is what causes death and conflict in the real world.

Keep referring back to the question.

Try to work quotes into your sentences.

Conclusion

6

The open-minded narrator of 'The Right Word' is able to consider things from a different point of view and finds her life benefits because of it. The arrogant hawk in 'Hawk Roosting' cannot do this. The difference in viewpoint between the two poems shows that conflict can be avoided by considering the feelings and attitudes of other people, as the narrator in 'The Right Word' does. In contrast, 'Hawk Roosting' shows that feelings of self-importance are likely to lead to conflict.

Make sure you've answered the question.

Sample Question 3

Here's your <u>third and final</u> Sample Question. You could try to come up with your <u>own rough plan</u> for an answer — remember, you can choose to write about <u>any other poem</u> from the cluster.

Here's Sample Question 3

Not much to say here. You should <u>know</u> what you're doing by now...

SAMPLE QUESTION 3

You're still being asked to <u>compare</u> the two poems.

You <u>must</u> write about this poem.

Question 3   <u>Compare</u> how conflict is presented in *The Charge of the Light Brigade* and <u>one other poem</u> in the 'Conflict' cluster.

Remember to compare:
- what kinds of conflict are shown
- how these conflicts are presented

Write about <u>one</u> other poem from 'Conflict' too.

Here's an Example Plan for Sample Question 3

Here's <u>another way</u> you could plan your answer. The table helps you sort out <u>which quotes</u> you want to use to <u>support each of the points</u> you make.

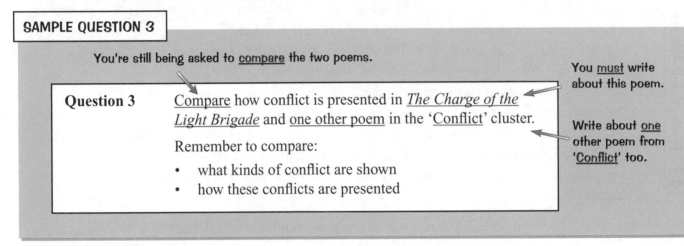

Poem 1: The Charge of the Light Brigade, Poem 2: Out of the Blue

	Poem 1	Poem 2
Intro: kind of conflict shown	Battle	results of terrorist attack
Conflict presented through language	scene of battle: "Into the valley of Death"	feelings of victim: "appalling"
Conflict presented through form and structure	Repetition, rhyme, rhythm: "Half a league, half a league, / Half a league onward"	repetition: "I am waving, waving"
Attitudes towards conflict	Praises soldiers: "Noble six hundred"	Sympathy for victim: "Does anyone see / a soul worth saving?"

Conclusion: sympathy for people in both poems

Always write about language, form and structure...

<u>Don't panic</u> — the question looks tricky at first but it's just like the other questions you've seen. Remember to keep comparing the language, form and structure of both poems and you'll be fine.

THIS IS A FLAP.
FOLD THIS PAGE OUT.

How to Answer the Question

Form and Structure — **3**

energy of the battle. The Light Brigade's charge towards its death is emphasised by the repetition in the first two lines of the poem: "half a league, / Half a league onward...". The weapons they are faced with are also repeated, e.g. "Cannon to right of them, / Cannon to left of them", to emphasise the danger faced by the cavalry and the bravery of the men. Armitage also uses repetition to suggest an inevitable ending. In 'Out of the Blue', actions like "waving, waving" and "tiring, tiring" are repeated — this shows us how hopeless the narrator's situation has become. The tone of the poem becomes more desperate towards the end as the narrator himself loses hope of survival.

Write about how features like form and structure create an effect.

Feelings and Attitudes — **4**

The narrator of 'Out of the Blue' addresses the reader directly. He pleads, "So when will you come?", but we are helpless. We stand and watch, but can do nothing to save him. This suggests how newspapers and television often make us feel like helpless witnesses to tragedies like September 11th. Tennyson, on the other hand, wrote 'The Charge of the Light Brigade' as a rousing description of a tragic but brave sacrifice: "Honour the Light Brigade, / Noble six hundred!" The final exclamation mark emphasises the poem's message — that we should celebrate these men. Although the order given to the Light Brigade was doubtful, we are shown that doubt did not get in the way of honour and the soldiers' sense of duty.

Write about how the poem makes you feel.

Show that you understand the message of the poem.

Conclusion — **5**

Both 'The Charge of the Light Brigade' and 'Out of the Blue' deal with conflict, but their messages are very different. Tennyson wants us to enthusiastically "Honour the Light Brigade" and remember how brave they were. We also sympathise with the narrator in 'Out of the Blue' who is "trying and trying" to survive, but his death is presented as sad and desperate instead of honourable.

Make sure your conclusion answers the question.

How to Answer the Question

Here's a 'C' grade sample answer to the exam question on p. 62.

Compare how conflict is presented in 'The Charge of the Light Brigade' and one other poem in the 'Conflict' cluster.

Remember to compare:
* what kinds of conflict are shown
* how these conflicts are presented

Introduction 1

Conflict often has harmful effects, like death and destruction, so it is usually looked at negatively. However, conflict can also bring out positive traits in people, and the people involved in it may be respected. 'The Charge of the Light Brigade' and 'Out of the Blue' deal with different types of conflict, and leave the reader with very different impressions of the people involved in it. 'The Charge of the Light Brigade' describes an incident during the Crimean War and reflects on the obedience of soldiers and army discipline. 'Out of the Blue' looks at conflict from the point of view of a victim of the September 11th terrorist attacks — it describes the growing panic of being close to death and the powerlessness of onlookers.

Start making comparisons as early as possible.

Briefly outline what the poems are about in the intro.

Language 2

The language used in 'Out of the Blue' reflects the terrible situation the narrator is in, as well as his determination to live. Despite the chaos, he insists that "the white of surrender is not yet flying." We know that his hope is misplaced though. He sees the depth beneath him as "appalling" — the repetition of this word emphasises how impossible his situation is. In 'The Charge of the Light Brigade' there is also a sense of determination, but here it is a whole regiment rather than an individual. The "six hundred" and their commanding officer follow their orders without question because "Theirs not to reason why". They see that the situation they face is very dangerous, but their duty is clear. The soldiers ride "Into the valley of Death", which shows that they were brave enough to face an extremely dangerous situation. It also seems to criticise the officers who gave the order that would lead to the loss of so many lives.

Don't forget to use quotes.

Try to explain the effects of particular images.

The form and structure of the poems also play a part in getting the message across to the reader. 'The Charge of the Light Brigade' has a powerful rhythm and rhyme scheme that suggests the

The Controlled Assessment

If you're following Route B of the AQA English Literature course, you'll have to do a controlled assessment task for Unit 5: Exploring Poetry. That's what this page is about.

This is How Unit 5 Works

1) Your teacher will set you a question on some poetry. They might decide to use poems from the poetry Anthology that's covered in this book.

2) The question will ask you to compare contemporary poems (like those in Section 2) with ones from the Literary Heritage (Section 1).

3) You might have to listen to or watch performances of the poems and write about them in your answer.

> You'll be able to choose which poems to write about from the ones you've studied.

4) You're expected to write around 2000 words. Your answer is worth 25% of your final GCSE grade.

You're Allowed to Plan Your Answer First

1) You'll be able to spend time in class planning and preparing for this essay.

2) During this time, you'll be allowed to look at books and the Internet and ask your teacher questions. You must make a note of anything you use to help you (e.g. a website) in a bibliography.

3) You can write a rough draft if you want, but you won't be able to have it with you while you're writing up your answer. You can take in brief notes though.

You'll Have up to Four Hours to Write Up Your Answer

1) You can write up your answer in your classroom over a few lessons, but you'll be under exam conditions.

2) You'll be given unmarked copies of the poems to help you.

For Sam's control assessment he had to demonstrate skilful changing of channels.

3) You can write up your essay by hand, or type it up on a computer.

> You'll be allowed a dictionary or to use your spell-check, but if you do have a computer you won't be able to get on the Internet.

4) Your work will be collected in at the end of every session. When you've finished, your teacher will collect in everything you've written — including any drafts you did earlier on.

You'll write up the task under exam conditions...

So, your teacher will set you a question on some poems you've studied. You'll have time to prepare your answer, but you're expected to write it up in a maximum of four supervised hours.

The Controlled Assessment

I expect you'd find it helpful to know what <u>kind of questions</u> you're going to get asked, how best to <u>approach</u> them and what you'll be <u>marked</u> on. So I've done a nice page about it for you.

You'll Be Marked on Three Main Things

<u>Whatever</u> question you get, you'll get marks for doing these <u>three</u> things.

Keep them in mind when you're <u>planning</u> and <u>writing</u> your answer.

① Giving your own <u>thoughts</u> and <u>opinions</u> on the poems and supporting the points you make with <u>quotes</u> from the text.

② <u>Explaining</u> the effects of features like <u>form</u>, <u>structure</u> and <u>language</u>.

③ Describing the <u>similarities</u> and <u>differences</u> between poems.

This means you should always <u>compare</u> the poems you're writing about.

Here Are Some Example Questions

EXAMPLE QUESTION 1

Compare the different ways conflict is presented in a range of contemporary and Literary Heritage poems.

EXAMPLE QUESTION 2

Explore how the poems you have studied use structure and language to describe conflicts.

1) You can <u>choose</u> which poems you write about, but you <u>must</u> include <u>at least</u> <u>one contemporary</u> and <u>one Literary Heritage</u> poem. The number of poems you write about is <u>up to you</u>, but make sure you have <u>plenty to say</u> about each one.

2) Even if the question doesn't specifically ask you to <u>compare</u> the poems, that's what you <u>have to do</u> to get good marks.

Think About How You're Going to Tackle the Question

The question you get might be quite <u>general</u>, so you're going to have to think about the <u>best way</u> to approach it. You might find it <u>helpful</u> to start off with a <u>basic plan</u> covering the things below.

- Choose poems which relate to the <u>theme</u> of the question.
- Look at the <u>language</u> — what effect does it create? <u>How</u> does it do this?
- Look at the <u>form and structure</u> — what effect do they create? <u>How</u> do they do this?
- What are the <u>feelings and attitudes</u> in the poems?

How do the poems <u>compare</u> with each other?

Prepare your answer carefully...

The question is set by your teacher, but you'll always be <u>marked</u> in the <u>same way</u>. Always write about <u>language</u>, <u>form</u> and <u>structure</u>, as well as the <u>feelings and attitudes</u> in the poems.

The Controlled Assessment

A <u>good plan</u> will help you organise your thoughts and write a <u>clear</u>, <u>well-structured</u> essay — which means lots of <u>lovely marks</u>. And the good news is, you'll have <u>plenty of time</u> to prepare one.

Choose Your Poems and Map Out Ideas

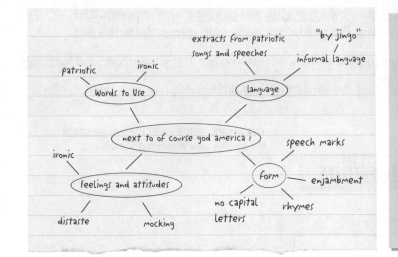

1) Let's say that for <u>Example Question 1</u> on page 65, you decide to write about <u>next to of course god america i</u>.

2) You might want to <u>map out</u> your <u>ideas</u> like on the left, so you can decide what to include in your detailed <u>plan</u>.

3) It's a good idea to do this for <u>all</u> your poems and make <u>links</u> between them.

4) Write down some <u>key quotes</u> you want to include in your essay too.

Write a Detailed Plan

Here's an <u>example plan</u> for Question 1 on the last page. You can make it fairly <u>detailed</u>, as you've got enough time.

For some ideas on different ways to plan, see page 56.

Introduction
Key points of essay
Different views of conflict

Feelings and Attitudes
* Light Brigade — duty, honour
* Right Word — fear, kindness
* Flag — anger, irony
* next to of course — irony

Language
* Light Brigade — patriotic — "Noble six hundred"
* Right Word — uncertain — "Is that the wrong description?"
* Flag — questioning, defining — "It's just a piece of cloth"
* next to of course — patriotic, ironic — "heroic happy dead"

Form and Structure
* Light Brigade — formal, drives forward, rhymes
* next to of course — ignores sentence rules, rhymes
* Right Word — short stanzas, punctuation
* Flag — questions, rhymes, ends with rhyming couplet

Conclusion
* All have different views of conflict.
* 'Light Brigade' is a tribute, 'Flag' and 'next to of course' talk about the dangers of patriotism, 'Right Word' tries to avoid conflict

Plan what you're going to write about before you start...

Use your preparation time <u>wisely</u> to come up with a <u>good plan</u> for your essay. You won't be allowed it with you when you're writing up, but you can have a <u>few notes</u> to jog your memory.

The Controlled Assessment

Here are some grade 'C' paragraphs from a sample answer to Example Question 1 on page 65.

Here's a Sample Introduction

Write an introduction that makes it clear you've understood the question, like this one:

> Poets write about all kinds of different themes, including conflict. Each poet has a different view of conflict because everyone has their own experiences in life, and their opinions come across in their poems. Tennyson's 'The Charge of the Light Brigade' is obviously about the bravery of the soldiers, but the message of 'next to of course god america i' is less clear. Imtiaz Dharker's 'The Right Word' is full of doubt and uncertainty, while 'Flag' suggests that being a good person is more important than being patriotic.

Tell the reader the names of the poems you're going to discuss.

Here are Some Sample Paragraphs

You've got 2000 words, so try to write about the poems in detail.

> 'The Right Word' has a first-person narrator who feels scared and threatened. The narrator tries to label the person outside using words like "terrorist", "freedom-fighter" and "guerrilla warrior", but she keeps finding problems with every word she thinks of. She asks: "Is that the wrong description?" Eventually she realises that she is wasting her time and that words are not as important as being kind and treating everyone equally, which is why she invites the stranger in to eat with her and her family.

Use quotes from the poem that fit in with what you're saying.

Back up your ideas with evidence from the poem.

It's important to give your own opinions on the poems. You'll sound more convincing if you give plenty of evidence to support your ideas — this means using lots of quotes.

> 'next to of course god america i' has a subtle meaning. At first it seems to be a patriotic poem because it has quotes from patriotic songs, but mentioning death reminds us that conflict has negative effects. Not using capital letters for "god" and "america" suggests that the poem is mocking people who are patriotic, and this is also suggested when the speaker makes mistakes like saying "by gorry" instead of "by golly". It seems as though the poet is trying to make fun of people who say things like that. The poem has an ironic tone, which is obvious in lines like "they did not stop to think they died instead". The poet seems to be suggesting that it is not a good idea to die for your country without thinking about what you are doing. There is a contrast with 'The Charge of the Light Brigade', because Tennyson praises the Light Brigade for their bravery in dying for their country.

Keep focused on the theme of the question.

Use quotes to support your ideas.

Remember to compare the poems.

Making Comparisons

This is the stuff you'll <u>really</u> need to know — how to <u>compare</u> two poems.

Comparing Means Finding Similarities and Differences

1) Comparing means looking at <u>two</u> or more things <u>together</u>.

2) You need to make <u>links</u> between the two poems.
<u>Don't</u> just write about <u>one poem</u> then the <u>other</u>.

3) Explain <u>how</u> the two poems are <u>similar</u> and <u>different</u>.

4) Give <u>examples</u> and <u>quotes</u> to back up your ideas.

Different children,
same terrible hat.

Questions Use Key Words to Help You

One of the questions in the exam could ask you to <u>compare</u> the way <u>conflict</u> is <u>presented</u> in two poems. The question might <u>look</u> a bit like this:

> 1 [Compare] the ways that conflict is presented in *Hawk Roosting* and [one other poem] from 'Conflict'.
>
> Remember to compare:
> • the types of conflict in the poems
> • how the conflict is [presented]

Write about similarities AND differences.

Choose a poem that goes well with 'Hawk Roosting'.

Talk about <u>how</u> the poets show us the conflict.

When you've <u>read</u> the question, you need to work out <u>how</u> to answer it:

1) <u>Choose</u> another poem that <u>links</u> well with the one in the question.

2) <u>Link</u> the poems together by describing their <u>similarities</u> and <u>differences</u>.

3) You can <u>compare</u> feelings, structure, language and ideas.

4) Make a <u>plan</u> showing <u>how</u> you want to compare the poems (see p.56).

Try to Compare the Texts as you Go Along

Here's part of a <u>sample answer</u> to the question above, comparing '<u>Hawk Roosting</u>' with '<u>The Falling Leaves</u>'.

'Hawk Roosting' and 'The Falling Leaves' [both] use natural images to describe conflict. In 'Hawk Roosting' the narrator is a hawk who describes killing its prey as though it is something exciting and positive. 'The Falling Leaves', [on the other hand,] uses images of falling leaves and snowflakes to express sadness about lives lost in war.

This word introduces a similarity.

This phrase shows that the answer is comparing both poems <u>directly</u>.

Look at the next page for more linking words.

Compare the poems by finding links between them...

There's a fair bit to remember when you're <u>comparing</u> poems, but this section should help a bit. Have a look at the next page for some more handy <u>linking words</u> for your comparison essays.

Linking Words

Another trick you need to <u>practise</u> is using <u>linking words</u>. These are the lovely helpful words that link <u>different points</u> of your essay <u>together</u> and help you make comparisons.

You Need to Link Different Points Together

1) Don't just jump from one point to the next — <u>structure</u> your essay.

2) Use <u>linking words</u> to show when you're comparing.

3) <u>Learn</u> a few linking words for talking about <u>similarities</u> and some for describing the <u>differences</u> between poems.

4) Use words like 'therefore' and 'so' for <u>conclusions</u>.

You gotta link stuff together.

Use These Words for Describing Similarities...

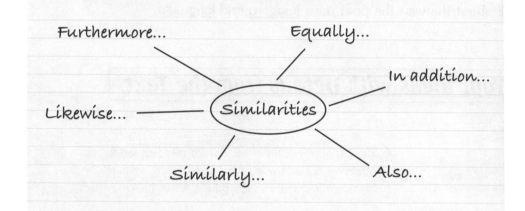

Furthermore... Equally... In addition... Likewise... Similarities Similarly... Also...

...and These Ones for Differences

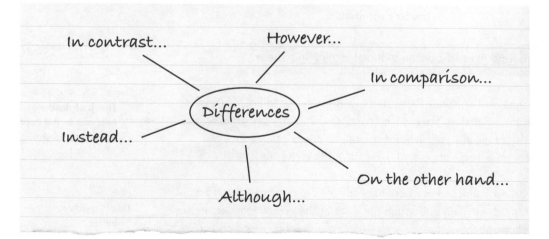

In contrast... However... In comparison... Differences Instead... On the other hand... Although...

Furthermore, some linking words are also equally similar...

<u>Learn</u> the words on this page and <u>when</u> to use them in your essays. It's a good idea to make it <u>clear</u> to the examiner whether you're talking about <u>similarities</u> or <u>differences</u> between the poems.

Quoting

Don't just jot down any old <u>stuff</u> — you've got to <u>back it up</u> to get the marks.

"One loves to quote."

You Need to Back Up Your Argument

Writing a good essay is about <u>backing up</u> your points with <u>proper evidence</u>.
There are <u>two ways</u> to back up your points:

1) <u>QUOTING</u>   <u>Quoting</u> means giving <u>examples</u> from a poem in the <u>exact same words</u> as the original. When you quote something, you have to explain <u>how</u> it <u>backs up</u> your argument.

2) <u>EXAMPLES</u>   You can talk about what happens in the poem in your <u>own words</u>. You can make <u>quick points</u> when you <u>haven't</u> got <u>time</u> to quote loads of stuff.

The <u>best</u> way to back up your points is to use <u>direct quotations</u> from the poem.
That way you can also talk about the way the poet uses <u>imagery</u> and <u>language</u>.

Always Support Your Ideas with Details from the Text

Here are some quoting <u>top tips</u>:

1) **Make sure the quote is <u>relevant</u>.**

✓ The narrator in 'Out of the Blue' is pleading for our attention: "Does anyone see / a soul worth saving?" He is terrified and wonders if he is worth being rescued.

✗ The character in 'Out of the Blue' asks a powerful question: "So when will you come? / Do you think you are watching, watching / a man shaking crumbs / or pegging out washing?"

This bit's not needed.

2) <u>Don't</u> quote <u>large chunks</u> of text — it just wastes time.

3) <u>Don't</u> write <u>long lists</u> of quotes without <u>explaining</u> them.

✗ Each stanza of 'The Yellow Palm' starts with the repeated line, "As I made my way down Palestine Street". The narrator then describes what he did: "I watched a funeral pass", "I heard the call to prayer" and "I met two blind beggars". These are everyday events in the life of the city.

This just describes what happens in the poem — there's nothing original.

✓ In 'The Yellow Palm', scenes of ordinary city life are ruined by the effects of violent conflict. Looking in through the door of the golden mosque, we see the people worshipping, but we are warned that there is "blood on the walls". There are lots of images connecting everyday life with sadness in this poem.

This is much better.

Make sure you explain what the quote means...

Quotes. Can't live with 'em, can't live without 'em, as I believe the saying goes. Or a saying anyway. Think <u>carefully</u> about which ones to use and where, that's my advice. <u>Sorted</u>.

Structure

You need to know <u>why</u> paragraphs are so important — and also how to write a <u>good one</u>.

Structure Your Answer by Using Paragraphs

You need to <u>organise</u> your points clearly and <u>link</u> them together. The best way to do that is to write in <u>paragraphs</u>. Use a <u>paragraph</u> for each point in your answer. Here are a few ways to <u>link</u> your paragraphs together:

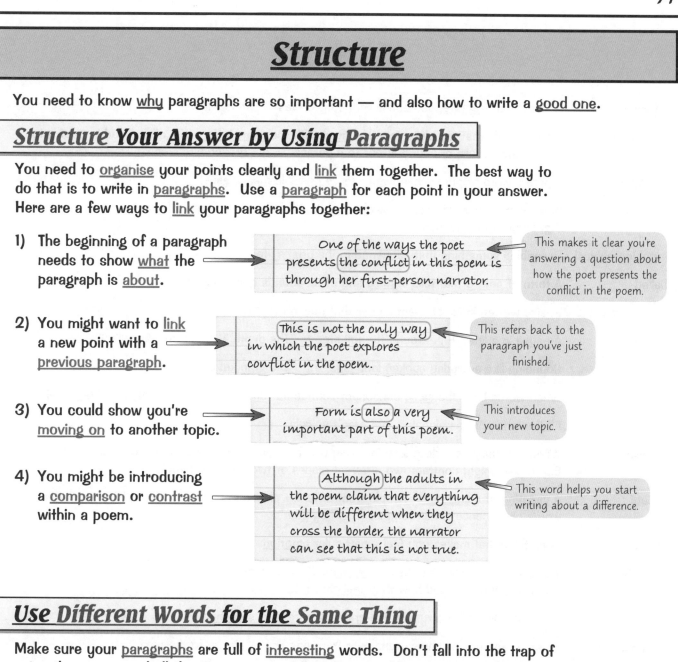

1) The beginning of a paragraph needs to show <u>what</u> the paragraph is <u>about</u>.

> One of the ways the poet presents the conflict in this poem is through her first-person narrator.

This makes it clear you're answering a question about how the poet presents the conflict in the poem.

2) You might want to <u>link</u> a new point with a <u>previous paragraph</u>.

> This is not the only way in which the poet explores conflict in the poem.

This refers back to the paragraph you've just finished.

3) You could show you're <u>moving on</u> to another topic.

> Form is also a very important part of this poem.

This introduces your new topic.

4) You might be introducing a <u>comparison</u> or <u>contrast</u> within a poem.

> Although the adults in the poem claim that everything will be different when they cross the border, the narrator can see that this is not true.

This word helps you start writing about a difference.

Use Different Words for the Same Thing

Make sure your <u>paragraphs</u> are full of <u>interesting</u> words. Don't fall into the trap of using the same word all the time — especially adjectives like "<u>nice</u>" or "<u>weird</u>".

> The narrator of 'Out of the Blue' is very scared. He's scared because he's trapped in a burning building and can't escape. He sounds scared because of the scared language he uses.

It may be 'correctly' written, but it's not going to score you many points because it's so <u>boring</u>.

This is loads better. Using lots of different adjectives makes your answer more <u>interesting</u>.

> The narrator of 'Out of the Blue' is very scared. He is terrified because he's trapped in a burning building and can't escape. He sounds anxious because of the fearful language he uses.

Pizza is nice, chocolate is nice, exams are NOT very nice...

Imagine how <u>dull</u> your essays will sound if you keep using the <u>same</u> old words all the time. Try to <u>vary</u> your sentences a bit so they sound more <u>interesting</u>. Your answer will sound loads <u>better</u>.

Glossary

adjective	A word that <u>describes</u> something, e.g. "big", "fast", "annoying".
alliteration	Where words that are close together <u>start</u> with the <u>same letter</u>. It's often used in poetry to give a nice pattern or sound effect to a phrase. E.g. "<u>b</u>roken <u>b</u>ird's egg".
ambiguity	Where a word or phrase has <u>two or more</u> possible <u>meanings</u>.
assonance	When words share the same <u>vowel sound</u> but the consonants are different. E.g. "bl<u>o</u>cked with st<u>o</u>ps".
autobiographical	Describing something that happened in the <u>poet's life</u>.
ballad	A form of <u>poetry</u> that tells a <u>story</u> and often sounds quite <u>musical</u>.
blank verse	Poetry written in iambic pentameter that <u>doesn't rhyme</u>.
caesura	A <u>pause</u> in a line. E.g. around the full stop in "The depth is appalling. Appalling".
colloquial	Sounding like everyday <u>spoken</u> language, e.g. "We grabbed a drink".
consonance	When words have the <u>same</u> consonant sounds but <u>different</u> vowel sounds, e.g. "<u>tall</u> / <u>toil</u>".
consonants	All the letters in the alphabet that <u>aren't vowels</u>.
contrast	When two things are described in a way which emphasises <u>how different</u> they are. E.g. a poet might contrast two different places or two different people.
dialect	A <u>variation</u> of a <u>language</u>. People from different places or backgrounds might use different words or sentence constructions. E.g. "by gum".
emotive	Something that makes you <u>feel</u> a particular <u>emotion</u>.
empathy	When someone feels like they <u>understand</u> what someone else is experiencing and how they <u>feel</u> about it.
end-stopping	Finishing a line of poetry with the <u>end</u> of a <u>phrase or sentence</u>.
enjambment	When a sentence or phrase runs over from <u>one line</u> or <u>stanza</u> to the <u>next</u>.
first person	When someone writes about themselves, or a group which includes them, using words like "<u>I</u>", "<u>my</u>" and "<u>me</u>".
form	The <u>type</u> of poem, e.g. a sonnet or a ballad, and its <u>features</u>, like rhyme, rhythm, metre.
free verse	Poetry that <u>doesn't rhyme</u> and has <u>no regular rhythm</u>.
iambic pentameter	Poetry with a <u>metre</u> of <u>ten syllables</u> — five of them stressed, and five unstressed. The <u>stress</u> falls on <u>every second syllable</u>, e.g. "They <u>fell</u>, like <u>snow</u>flakes <u>wip</u>ing <u>out</u> the <u>noon</u>".
iambic tetrameter	Like iambic pentameter but with a metre of <u>eight</u> syllables — four stressed and four unstressed. E.g. "O <u>what</u> made <u>fat</u>uous <u>sun</u>beams <u>toil</u>".
imagery	Language that creates a <u>picture in your mind</u>. It includes <u>metaphors</u> and <u>similes</u>.
internal rhyme	When two words in the <u>same line</u> rhyme. E.g. "Sitting <u>alone</u> on a round flat <u>stone</u> on a hummock there".
irony	When <u>words</u> are used in a <u>sarcastic</u> or <u>comic</u> way to <u>imply the opposite</u> of what they normally mean. It can also mean when there is a big difference between <u>what people expect</u> and <u>what actually happens</u>.
language	The <u>choice of words</u> used. Different kinds of language have <u>different effects</u>.

Glossary

layout	The way a piece of poetry is visually presented to the reader, e.g. line length, whether the poem is broken up into different stanzas, whether lines create some kind of visual pattern.
metaphor	A way of describing something by saying that it is something else, to create a vivid image. E.g. "the china plate of a shoulder blade".
metre	The arrangement of stressed and unstressed syllables to create rhythm in a line of poetry.
monologue	One person speaking for a long period of time.
mood	The feel or atmosphere of a poem, e.g. humorous, threatening, eerie.
narrative	Writing that tells a story, e.g. the poem 'The Charge of the Light Brigade'.
narrator	The voice speaking the words that you're reading. E.g. 'At the Border, 1979' is written from the point of view of a young child, which means the young child is the poem's narrator.
oxymoron	A phrase which seems to contradict itself, because the words have meanings that don't seem to fit together, e.g. "heroic happy dead".
persona	A fictional character or identity adopted by a poet. Poets often create a persona so they can describe things from a different person's point of view, e.g. a male poet might use a female persona.
personification	A special kind of metaphor where you write about something as if it's a person with thoughts and feelings. E.g. "The kind old sun will know".
rhyme scheme	A pattern of rhyming words in a poem, e.g. in 'The Yellow Palm', the 2nd, 4th and 6th lines in each stanza rhyme.
rhyming couplet	A pair of rhyming lines that are next to each other, e.g. the last two lines of 'Flag'.
rhythm	A pattern of sounds created by the arrangement of stressed and unstressed syllables.
sibilance	Repetition of 's' and 'sh' sounds.
simile	A way of describing something by comparing it to something else, usually by using the words "like" or "as", e.g. "the world overflowing / like a treasure chest".
sonnet	A form of poem with fourteen lines, and usually following a clear rhyme scheme. There are different types of sonnets. They're often about love.
stanza	A group of lines in a poem. Stanzas can also be called verses.
structure	The order and arrangement of ideas and events in a piece of writing, e.g. how the poem begins, develops and ends.
syllable	A single unit of sound within a word. E.g. "all" has one syllable, "always" has two and "establishmentarianism" has nine.
symbolism	When an object stands for something else. E.g. a candle might be a symbol of hope, or a dying flower could symbolise the end of a relationship.
theme	An idea or topic that's important in a piece of writing. E.g. a poem could be based on the theme of war.
tone	The mood or feelings suggested by the way the narrator writes, e.g. confident, thoughtful.
voice	The personality narrating the poem. Poems are usually written either using the poet's voice, as if they're speaking to you directly, or the voice of a character.
vowels	The letters "a", "e", "i", "o" and "u".

Index

Index

next to of course god america i
14, 34, 40, 44, 46, 52

O

Out of the Blue 20, 41-43, 47-48
Owen, Wilfred 4

P

paragraphs 71
passive sentences 29
past and future 9
past and present 5, 23
patriotic language 15
patriotism 15, 34, 40, 52
personal experiences 41
personification 5, 17, 23
philosophical language 5
planning 56, 59, 62, 64, 66
poetic devices 45-46
poetry exam 54
politicians 34
Poppies 32, 35, 38, 41, 48, 53
Postgate Cole, Margaret 12
power 17

Q

questions 21
quotes 70

R

reality of battles 36
refrains 44
regrets 13
religion 34
repetition 7, 9, 19, 25, 27, 44-45
respect 13
rhetorical language 15, 19, 34, 46
rhyme 47
rhythm 47
Right Word, The 26, 39, 41, 45, 48

S

sadness 13, 23, 38, 53
sample answers 57, 60, 63, 67
sample questions 55, 59, 62
sarcasm 15
self-centred language 17
senses 25
Sheers, Owen 22
similes 51
Smith, Stevie 8
sonnets 44
spider diagrams 56, 66
structure 71
surreal language 9
suggested criticism 25
sympathy 5

T

tables 56
Tennyson, Alfred 6
tercets 44
terror 11
third-person narration 48
trapped 31

U

universal language 11
unreliable narrators 48
unusual vocabulary 46
use of first person 48

V

verbs 21
violence 7, 11, 17, 31, 51, 52
vivid descriptions 25

W

warnings 19
Weir, Jane 32
World Trade Centre 21

Y

Yellow Palm, The 24, 34, 39, 44, 47, 50

__Acknowledgements__

The Publisher would like to thank:

For poems:

John Agard: 'Flag' — From *Half Caste and Other Poems* by John Agard, first published in the UK by Hodder Children's, an imprint of Hachette Children's Books, 338 Euston Road, London, NW1 3BH

Simon Armitage: Extract from *Out of the Blue* — Enitharmon, 2008, reproduced by permission of Enitharmon

Ciaran Carson: 'Belfast Confetti' — By kind permission of the author and The Gallery Press, Loughcrew, Oldcastle, County Meath, Ireland from Collected Poems (2008)

E.E. Cummings: 'next to of course god america i' is reprinted from *COMPLETE POEMS 1904-1962*, by E.E. Cummings, edited by George J. Firmage, by permission of W.W. Norton & Company. Copyright © 1991 by the Trustees for the E.E. Cummings Trust and George James Firmage.

Imtiaz Dharker: 'The Right Word' — Imtiaz Dharker, *The Terrorist at my Table* (Bloodaxe Books, 2006)

Choman Hardi: 'At the Border, 1979' — Choman Hardi, *Life for Us* (Bloodaxe Books, 2004)

Ted Hughes: 'Bayonet Charge' — From *The Hawk in the Rain*, 9780571086146, Faber and Faber, first published 1957

Ted Hughes: 'Hawk Roosting' — From Lupercal Faber and Faber; Reprint of 1970 edition (8 Oct 1985) ISBN-13: 978-0571092468

Robert Minhinnick: 'The Yellow Palm' — from *King Driftwood* (Carcanet Press, 2008) reproduced by permission of Carcanet Press Ltd

Margaret Postgate Cole: 'The Falling Leaves' — From *Scars Upon My Heart* selected by Catherine Reilly (Virago, 1981), reproduced by permission of David Higham Associates

Owen Sheers: 'Mametz Wood' — Copyright © 2005 Owen Sheers. Reproduced by permission of the author c/o Rogers, Coleridge & White Ltd., 20 Powis Mews, London W11 1JN

Stevie Smith: 'Come On, Come Back' — Estate of James MacGibbon

Jane Weir: 'Poppies' — By kind permission of Templar Poetry on behalf of the author, 2009

For photographs:

John Agard, Simon Armitage, E.E. Cummings, Ted Hughes, Robert Minhinnick, Owen Sheers — Rex Features

Ciaran Carson — Elzbieta Lempp / The Gallery Press

Imtiaz Dharker — Simon Powell

Choman Hardi — Bloodaxe Books

Wilfred Owen — Lebrecht Music and Arts Photo Library / Alamy

Stevie Smith — Mary Evans Picture Library / Robin Adler

Alfred Tennyson — Mary Evans Picture Library

Jane Weir — Templar Poetry

Every effort has been made to locate copyright holders and obtain permission to reproduce poems and images. For those poems and images where it has been difficult to trace the originator of the work, we would be grateful for information. If any copyright holder would like us to make an amendment to the acknowledgements, please notify us and we will gladly update the book at the next reprint. Thank you.